Mongolian Culture and Society in the Age of Globalization

Mongolian Culture and Society in the Age of Globalization

Henry G. Schwarz
Editor

Western Washington University

Center for East Asian Studies
Western Washington University

Studies on East Asia, Volume 26
Mongolian Culture and Society in the Age of Globalization, edited by Henry G. Schwarz

The Center for East Asian Studies publishes scholarly works on topics relating to China, Japan, Korea, and Mongolia.

Mongolian Culture and Society in the Age of Globalization

Proceedings of an International Research Conference,
Western Washington University
August 5-6, 2005

Edited
by
Henry G. Schwarz

Center for East Asian Studies
Western Washington University
2006

Library of Congress Cataloging-in-Publication Data

Mongolian Culture and Society in the Age of Globalization:
Proceedings of an International Research Conference,
Western Washington University, August 5-6, 2005 / edited by
Henry G. Schwarz
x, 169 p. ; cm. -- (Studies on East Asia ; v. 26)
ISBN 0-914584-26-X

Manufactured in the United States of America

Contents

Preface

One of the most ubiquitous terms used over the past dozen years or more has been globalization, but there is no consensus as to its precise meaning. Instead we have been witnessing an ever growing number of definitions and descriptions offered by experts in such fields as economics, politics, anthropology and sociology. If they agree on anything at all, it seems that globalization has come about largely as the result of three factors: the end of the so-called cold war, the emergence of a new economic world order, and the ubiquitous use of electronic communications. As a result, what we have seen so far is that most studies of globalization have focused primarily on the phenomenon's political and economic modalities in general and almost always within the framework of "country studies." It was this dual emphasis both on political and economic events and on states that peaked my curiosity.

My initial surmise was that most writers on this subject may have been so impressed with the three main causes of globalization, itemized above, that they restricted their search for the effects of globalization to the same political, economic and technological arenas. This interpretation made me uncomfortable because one must assume that most of these writers are sufficiently knowledgeable so as not to confuse cause and effect and to know that a broad-gauged force like globalization is, by any measure, most certainly impacting all realms of human activity, including culture and society. One must, therefore, posit that there is some powerful force that is skewing research into globalization toward the political and economic. Indeed, we do not have to look far to find that force. It emanates from governments and some private organizations who offer substantial incentives in the form of grants, awards, memberships in "think tanks" and so on for work on political and economic subjects while doling out only a relative pittance for studies dealing with culture and society.

Moreover, even without such incentives it is almost always easier and less time-consuming to gather any kind of data within one country rather than within an area that straddles national boundaries. A key question, therefore, is whether research into an ethnic group's culture and society should always be at the country level and below. The temptation to do just that is great because of the just mentioned relative ease of gathering data and the fact that in many cases cultures and societies do coincide with political entities. Japanese culture and society are confined to Japan's political boundaries, and the same holds true for scores of other cases. But not for all; there are many ethnic groups that straddle state boundaries whose cultures and societies ought to be studied as single entities. Such an approach makes eminently good methodological sense because it also carries with it an additional benefit. Given the unquestionably great impact of governments and their policies on culture and society, as mentioned earlier, a study of globalization's impact on any culture and society in two adjacent states raises the possibility of not only reaching the primary goal of gauging the effects of globalization but also of getting at least a preliminary idea of the degree to which governmental policies influence the forces of globalization.

Mongolia is an excellent choice for studying the impact of globalization on culture and society for several reasons. One is that it is perhaps the most prominent case where a large cultural area is divided into two separate states. I will elaborate this point in my introduction. Another reason is presented by Shagdaryn Bira's chapter which goes back 800 years to the time of the Mongolian empire. Within less than one generation following its political birth in 1206, Mongolia became a world power. Several key elements of globalization today, such as the relatively free movement of goods, extensive cultural interchange over large areas of the globe, and the creation of a written language to serve as the official form of communication, were part and parcel of the Mongol world empire as well. This fact reminds us that globalization is not a brand-new phenomenon in human history and practically commands us to compare the two historical periods.

Finally, Mongolia is a good choice because of its enduring special relationship with China. In both historical periods, and indeed throughout recorded history, China's role has been of paramount importance to Mongolia because of its size and propinquity. In the political and military arenas, the differences between the two eras could not be starker. In the thirteenth century China was one of the five constituent parts of the Mongol world empire,[1] having had for the first time in its long history every square inch of its territory conquered by an outside force. Today, China governs half of ethnic Mongolia's territory and two-thirds of the world's Mongolian population.[2] It seems, therefore, highly advisable to include China in any investigation of Mongolian culture and society.

Having convinced myself that the time was ripe to start research on globalization's effect on culture and society and that ethnic Mongolia is one of the best places to start such research, I invited several Mongolists to join me in this new endeavor. I chose 2005 for our conference because it was the eve of the 800th anniversary of the creation of the Mongolian state and also the thirtieth anniversary of Mongolian Studies at Western Washington University. Much to my satisfaction, six Mongolists accepted my invitation, and we spent two memorable days last August intensively discussing globalization in Mongolia and critiquing each other's papers. The result of that conference lies before you.

It gives me great pleasure to acknowledge the generous financial assistance by the Office of the Provost of Western Washington University, the Henry G. Schwarz Endowment Fund for Mon-

[1] The four other parts were Chagatai in Central Asia, the Ilkhanate in Persia, the Golden Horde in Eastern Europe, and the Mongolian homeland.

[2] One could also include the rapid rise in China's present economic dominance, but I do not think the economic differences between the two historical periods are as dramatic as the political and military ones.

`golian Studies, the Chinggis Khan Foundation, the Embassy of Mongolia in the United States, and the Libraries and the Center for East Asian Studies at Western Washington University. I should also like to thank Marian Alexander, Catherine Barnhart, Tamara Belts, Béla Foltin, Jennie Huber, Connie Mallison, Margaret McFadyen, Rick Osen, Wayne Richter, and Kathleen Tomlonovic for helping out, in large ways and small. Without the timely and unstinting support by these individuals and organizations this conference and this book would not have been possible.

Henry G. Schwarz

Bellingham
May 1, 2006

Introduction: Some Conceptual Remarks

Henry G. Schwarz

My contribution to our common endeavor is quite modest. Aside from editing this book, I will attempt in this introduction to offer a few general conceptual remarks about culture, society and globalization and how they apply to Mongolia. Torrents of ink have been spilled over each of these three concepts, so much so in fact that everyone seems to have his own take on them. As the authors in this volume embark on a pioneering effort to explore the linkages between culture, society and globalization in Mongolia, I believe it is important to get back to basics and try to describe these three terms as precisely and economically as possible. I should like to say that my remarks are not intended to be guidelines for this conference or this book, but rather it is my hope that they may help stake out the parameters of future research into the subject of globalization and its effect on Mongolian culture and society.

To start out with, by culture I mean a complex of objects and values that affects a person's sense of identity with a group or society. It is, therefore, clear that culture and society are inextricably intertwined. One cannot exist without the other. In the broadest sense, culture is a society's way of life, and conversely, any society is the arena in which culture resides. It is identified by race, ethnicity, language, religion, or other social categories or groupings.

Cultures and societies have both temporal and spatial dimensions. There is little disagreement about their temporal dimensions.

We all know that what is understood as Mongolian culture today was not the same at any time in the past, and the same holds true for society. However, one does not always find the same unanimity of opinion when it comes to the spatial dimensions of cultures and societies. While there is common agreement that the size of a society can range from very small, such as a street gang, to all of humanity, that agreement sometimes disappears when analysis of a society and its culture is focused at a level that straddles political borders.

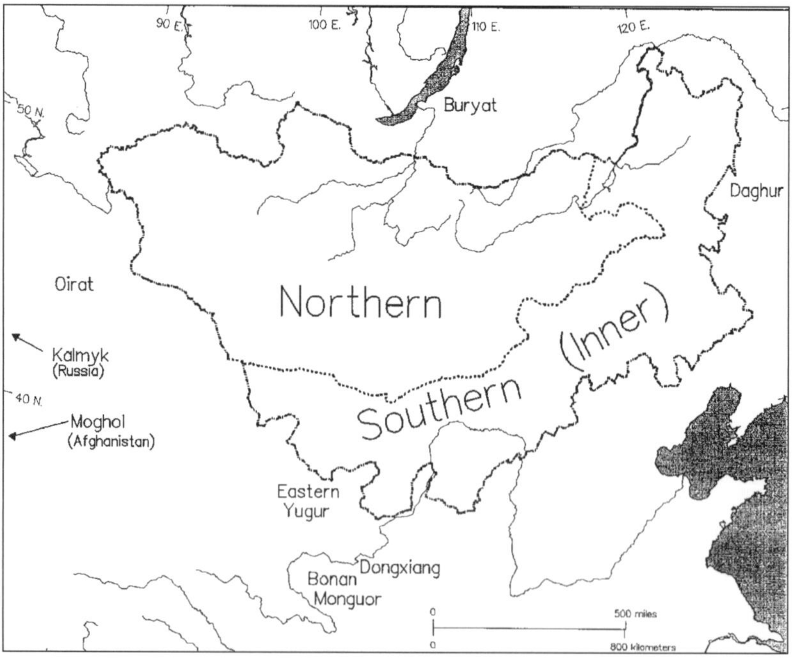

Mongolia

(Adapted from Henry G. Schwarz, *Mongolia and the Mongols : Holdings at Western Washington University* (Bellingham: Western Washington University, 1992), frontispiece).

Mongolia is a case in point. Among the several dozen of transnational cultural areas on this planet, there is perhaps none more suitable for gauging globalizations's impact on culture and society than Mongolia. In the first place, Mongolia in any sense of the word other than political/economic is much larger than the country by that name. When one focuses on cultural matters such as ethnicity and language -- in my considered opinion more important than political matters because they are much more enduring -- one discovers that Mongolia covers a huge area stretching from the Russian border to the Ordos Bend of the Yellow River and from the Xing'an Mountains in the east to the Altai Mountains in the west.[1]

When one speaks of one Mongolian culture and society from Lake Baikal to the Ordos, many people of different walks of life, even some Mongolists, instantly object that almost a century of political separation between the state in the north and the Chinese-administered southern part has created two Mongolian cultures and two Mongolian societies. The interesting thing is that advocates of this view readily agree that Mongolian culture and society can be fruitfully investigated at lower levels but most of them find it very difficult to acknowledge publicly the existence of one Mongolian culture and society stretching from Lake Baikal to the Ordos. Moreover, there was a time not long ago when native residents of ethnic Mongolia were pressured by their respective governments to keep quiet on this subject, and even today, although political controls have been greatly relaxed on both sides of the border, public acknowledgment of one ethnic Mongolia is still viewed as politically incorrect by many Mongols both north and south.

In order to place this deplorable state of affairs in its proper historical context, we need not go any farther back than the beginning of Mongolia's present political division which occurred when the Manchu dynasty fell in early 1912,[2] less than a century ago. For

---

1 It is rarely possible to completely match a political entity with a cultural entity, and our map is no exception. It combines the current political boundaries of the Mongolian state in the north with Chinese-administered Southern, or Inner, Mongolia. By doing so, it includes large numbers of Chinese within the southern border and a Kazakh minority in the northwestern corner but leaves out Mongols living beyond the northern and southwestern borders. On the other hand, unlike almost any other map in print today, it includes practically the entire contiguous area of cultural Mongolia.

2 During the time of the Manchu empire (1644-1911), there were administrative divisions within Mongolia, just as there were in the other countries and territories taken over by the Manchus, like China, Tibet, and later Dzungaria and East-

the next eight years, called the period of autonomy, the northern part of Mongolia succeeded in establishing a rump state with some of the trappings of sovereignty including a limited degree of foreign relations., but that changed all too soon.

Meanwhile, the southern part of Mongolia, often referred to as Inner Mongolia, with more than twice the number of Mongols than in the northern part, was unable to resist the attacks throughout the 1910s by a succession of Chinese warlords in Beijing who masqueraded as the Republic of China. As a result, the southern part of Mongolia has eventually become completely integrated into the political and economic framework of China.

Toward the end of the 1910s, a Chinese warlord clique then in control of Beijing made an attempt to annex the northern part of Mongolia and might have actually succeeded in its land grab had it not been for an entirely unforeseen event. The civil war in Russia had steadily moved eastward, bringing to northern Mongolia first troops under the command of Baron Sternberg and then, hard on their heels, the ultimately victorious Red Army. This event had two effects. The immediate result was that Chinese troops were chased home and prevented the warlords and their various successors from trying again. The second effect was that with the naming of the northern portion of Mongolia a "people's republic" in 1924, a process began that over the next seventy years completely subordinated the territory to policies made in Moscow. They affected not only the political, economic, and military fortunes of Mongols living in this rump state but, most relevant to our discussion, also the Mongols' view of their own culture and society.

Stalin and his colleagues were well aware of the strong sense of ethnic identity among all Mongols and the fact that more than two-third of them lived beyond Moscow's control in China. Stalin feared that these Mongols might be used by China or some third country to undermine his hold over the newly created rump state in the North.[3] The Soviet leaders sought to solve this perceived

---

ern Turkestan. The important point is that Mongolia was governed *in toto* by the central Manchu government through its Lifan Yuan.

[3] This fear was not as far-fetched as it had first appeared because after invading China, the Japanese created an autonomous Mongolian state under Demchug-

problem in two major ways. They sought to reorient Mongolian culture through close integration with the Soviet Union and its East European allies. The results included higher education for Mongols mostly in institutions in those countries, fluency in Russian, the adoption of the Cyrillic script, and the introduction of Western art forms, notably European opera.[4] Moreover, the Soviet leaders drastically reinterpreted Mongolian history and culture both in the classroom as well as among the general Mongolian population. The greatest embodiment of a unified Mongolia, Chinggis Khan, practically became an unperson. When he was portrayed at all, it was always in the darkest hues.[5] It was not only political leaders like Chinggis Khan who became all but banned but also major cultural figures, especially those who lived beyond the latter-day borders of the Mongolian People's Republic (MPR). For instance, I know of no book by or about Injannasi (1837-1892), arguably the greatest Mongolian literary figure of the nineteenth century and native of southern Mongolia,[6] that was published in the MPR during its lifetime, 1924-1991. The Soviet leadership also banned the use of clan names, thereby hoping to weaken an

---

dongrub which they hoped would, *inter alia*, be attractive to the Mongols in the MPR.

4 The Buriat and Kalmyk Mongols, as citizens of the Soviet Union, had of course already been Russified, but the Soviet leadership would go even so far as to remove the word "Mongolian" from the official name Buriat-Mongolian ASSR.

5 Another probable reason for the Soviets' degrading of Chinggis Khan, accompanied by a drastic deemphasis on the entire period of the Mongol world empire, was their desire to obscure the fact that the Mongols had conquered Russia. The Chinese, also conquered by the Mongols, had a different "solution" to the same problem. They declared Chinggis Khan and his successors Chinese emperors and gave the Chinese portion of the Mongol world empire a thoroughly Chinese name, Yuan.

6 Following in the footsteps of his father, Wangcugbala (1795-1847), and elder brother, Güleransa (1820-1855?), both well-known literary figures, Injannasi produced many works of poetry and prose that resonated well with literate Mongols during his time and for many generations to come. His most famous work is his historical novel, *Köke sudur*, which continues to be hugely popular in southern Mongolia, as evidenced by a continuous stream of books about the book and its author, as well as at least one feature movie and a book of cartoons.

awareness of common roots with the majority of their fellow Mongols who lived under Chinese administration.[7]

This policy of grossly distorting the Mongols' cultural and historical heritage, relentlessly carried out over many decades, eventually resulted in a wide-spread belief among the citizens of the Mongolian People's Republic that they were the only "real" Mongols and the other two-thirds, living under Chinese administration, were *erliiz* or half-breeds.[8] For the past decade or so, the government of the northern part of Mongolia, officially called Mongol Uls or simply Mongolia, has taken great strides to change its sovereignty from nominal to actual by establishing direct political and economic relations with scores of other countries and joining dozens of international organizations. It has been much less energetic in its efforts to undo the gross misperceptions that had been inculcated into generations of Mongols during the Soviet period.

With these few words about Mongolian culture and society, we now turn to the force at the center of our investigation, globalization. At the most general level, we can say that it has been a phenomenon since the dawn of human civilization and can be described in the simplest possible terms as a process which introduces changes on a scale encompassing many cultures and societies. It does not necessarily denote a truly planetary scale because concepts like "the world" mean not only physical entities but are also mental constructs. A case in point is what is frequently referred to as the Mongol world empire. It was, of course, the largest contiguous political entity in human history yet, equally obviously, it did not cover the entire planet. This fact mattered little to the people directly involved, conquerors and conquered alike, because in their minds the empire did indeed encompass their "world."[9]

---

[7] One could also add the suppression of the Buddhist church. Although the main reason was internal politics, another motivation probably stemmed from the church's close connection with Inner Mongolia and, of course, Tibet.

[8] Discovering this attitude toward them was perhaps the greatest shock for Mongols from Southern Mongolia when they were first allowed to visit the Mongolian People's Republic.

[9] The term "world" is still being used in a less than planetary sense. One local example is the "world series" in North American baseball, a lingering testimony to the provincialism of an earlier age.

This difference between fact and imagination still exists but it has shrunk a great deal, and we must reckon with the possibility that for an ever increasing share of humanity this difference will eventually disappear altogether.

This leads us to define the term's relationship to the concepts of Westernization and modernization because many people treat these terms as being synonymous with globalization. They are based on the older terms of "Western" and "modern" which have been widely used for perhaps a century or more and would therefore appear to be both useful and accurate concepts. As we shall see in a moment, they are not very useful for our investigation of Mongolian culture and society in the age of globalization.

This may be surprising to some because both Western and modern are undeniably useful terms. The areas in which they are most useful are place for Western and time for modern. Western Mongolia, like the Western hemisphere, is an accurate place name. Modern Mongolian history, like modern times, if identified as a definite time period, can also be accepted as being accurate. Beyond place and time, however, both terms become much less useful.

The term Western, despite its relatively long use or perhaps because of it, has been widely misused. Today, one finds Mongols, especially younger ones, labeling certain cultural trends as "Western" because, as Peter Marsh suggests in his chapter, it presumably conveys a certain degree of prestige. It does not seem to matter to these young people that some trends had in fact originated in Korea or Japan. The term Western, when applied in a cultural or societal context, is also often less accurate than generally believed. It is most useful at the time an idea or object is created in, say, Pasadena or Paris, but the further one moves away from that time and place, the less precise or meaningful the term becomes.

The term modern is also less useful in any discussion of culture and society than many people assume. Like Western, the term modern is maximally useful only within an extremely short time frame. This is true even in fields where the term is said to have long-lasting significance.

Two such fields are medicine and history. We are all familiar with the juxtaposition of traditional versus modern medicine. One finds this distinction as much in Mongolia as in North America and Europe.[10] When we look a little closer at what is called traditional medicine in Mongolia we discover that it is not one solid piece of knowledge and practice but that it consists of several layers.[11] Much of it dates back to the time when Tibetan missionaries introduced to Mongolia large chunks of Tibetan culture, including a highly developed medical system,[12] but it has also an older layer containing in greatly modified form elements of earlier medical beliefs and practices, and it has added in recent decades a new layer of some foreign procedures, pharmaceuticals, and machinery. It would appear that as time went on the traditional/modern dichotomy gradually lost its initial acuity, and those who still insist on using it use it in less than objective ways. One can easily imagine that the early Tibetan missionaries and their Mongolian followers used this dichotomy in the same biased or prejudicial way that some of us use it today.

The case for using the term modern in Mongolian history turns out to be as weak as in medicine. Present historiographical convention decrees that modern Mongolian history began in 1921. If one wonders why, a comparison with its neighbor to the south will provide the answer because there the start of modern Chinese history is fixed at 1840. What these two dates have in common is that they mark the beginning of the intrusion of massive European political and military power that brought in its wake foreign beliefs and practices. But as in the case of medicine, in no time at all these foreign or "modern" elements began to be molded into forms by forces that were both native or "traditional" as well as even newer external ones. From that moment on, the dichotomy between traditional and modern weakened.

If the term modern, as I have tried to show, is not as useful for our understanding of culture and society, it follows that the pro-

---

[10] Occasionally, there is also the explicit or implicit claim that modern medicine is Western medicine, but one should dismiss such claim as a product of provincialism or jingoism.

[11] One can discover the very same layered look in European medicine, but that subject is beyond the scope of this book.

[12] Tibetan medicine, in turn, owes much to ayurvedic and other medical systems in India and beyond.

cess of modernization loses much of its alleged utility. When viewed objectively, the term modernization is essentially nothing more than another name for the continuous process of change which is inherent in the temporal dimensions of all cultures and societies.

As for the term Westernization, it is often used for partisan, i.e. non-scientific, purposes, as when it is praised or condemned as a powerful force destined, or threatening, to engulf all of humanity. Yet any sober analysis shows that so far that predicted outcome is far from certain, and evidence is mounting that Westernization may well metamorphose into an entirely new hybrid process. We see numerous examples of this transformation in music and the visual arts. Moreover, there are cultural currents originating outside the "West" that may or may not hybridize with "Western" cultural forms. The growing popularity of manga and animé in North America and the rise there in conversions to Buddhism, Islam and other "non-Western" religions and beliefs are but two examples.[13] Other cultural currents, originating and spreading outside the "West", may eventually also impact North America and Europe. One such recent example is hallyu, the Korean pop culture wave, which had a major impact on Southeast Asia in the 1990s and is now sweeping Japan. Each one of these non-Western cultural currents may become globalized, which is yet another way of proving that Westernization is not identical to globalization.

Finally, what are the forces that produce globalization? They can be both non-human[14] as well as products of human volition. We are all too familiar with the former type as we become ever more inundated with all kinds of electronic communicators. An example of the latter would be what is sometimes called globalism. It can be found throughout human history whenever political and other influential leaders entertained expansionist ideas.[15] Global-

---

13 There is at least one crosscurrent that has already led to new hybrid forms, to wit, in culinary matters.

14 Gadgets like cellular phones are made and used by humans, but the impetus they give toward globalization is autonomous.

15 One such expansionist idea was manifest destiny, first publicized in 1845, which declared that the United States was destined to expand to the Pacific Oc-

ism can be both the cause as well as the effect of globalization. Two recent examples will have to suffice. The messianic fervor of German political leaders in the 1930s, clearly aiming at becoming a world power, grew out of the notion of a mythical Aryan race. While this globalism was obviously the product of many complex historical trends, it was an *idee fixe* that failed to engender globalization, as hoped for by its creators. On the other hand, the christo-fascist[16] variant of globalism currently held by some people in the United States who see themselves as entitled to ignore legal constraints such as international laws and agreements appears to be predominantly the product of one of the major driving forces of today's globalization, namely the temporary military and technological ascendancy of the United States.

The Mongolian world empire provides an excellent test case for an earlier kind of globalism which is sometimes called tenggerism[17] and is perhaps best symbolized by the self-proclaimed role of the khan as the sole representative of heaven on earth. The crucial question is when tenggerism assumed its messianic role. Some will argue that it happened prior to 1206 or, put differently, that tenggerism, or Mongolian globalism if you wish, was the engine for the globalization that developed with the expansion of the Mongol world empire. I have argued obliquely elsewhere[18] that this interpretation is not only factually flawed but also, unfortunately and unintendedly, lends credence to the view held by peoples like the Chinese and the Europeans who were conquered by the

---

ean. Like many other expansionist ideas, it failed to grow into a full-fledged form of globalism, but perhaps the final word on this has yet to be written.

[16] A term coined by the American philosopher Eric Hoffer (1902-1983).

[17] See Sh. Bira's important contributions in his article "Tenggerism and Modern Globalism : A Retrospective Outlook on Globalisation," *Inner Asia* 5:2 (2003), 107-118; "Mongolian Tenggerism and Modern Globalism : A Retrospective Outlook on Globalism," *Journal of the Royal Asiatic Society*, 2004, 2-12; and his chapter in this book, "The Mongolian Ideology of Tenggerism and Khubilai Khan."

[18] See my "Otrar," *Olon Ulsyn Mongolch Erdêmtnii V Ikh Khural* (Ulaanbaatar, 1992), v. 3, 333-340; and "Otrar Revisited," in *Mongol Sudlalyn Ögüüllüüd = Essays on Mongol Studies* [Commemorative volume on the occasion of Academician Bira's 70th birthday], edited by Ts. Batbayar et al. (Ulaanbaatar : Olon Ulsyn Mongol Sudlalyn Kholboo, 1998), 195-208.

Mongols that the latter were nothing more than barbarians whose lust for conquest was unbridled and a priori.

As for globalization itself, I mentioned earlier the relatively free movement of goods and the extensive cultural interchange during the Mongol world empire period, considered key elements of today's globalization. However, there are some major differences, as one would expect across the span of some 800 years. There is, of course, the already mentioned greater spatial dimension today as well as a much more intense process, both in physical and psychological ways. Perhaps most importantly, what distinguishes today's globalization from its forerunner in the thirteenth century is connectivity[19] by which I mean not only a physical two-way street, such as increasingly intensive electronic communications, but also a mindset that makes people feel much closer to those with whom they communicate or about whom them learn electronically. To paraphrase a well-known slogan in North America, a rapidly increasing number of people in all parts of the planet now "act globally and think locally."

I will conclude my remarks with a few suggested ways in which Mongolists may continue the lines of inquiry the contributors to this book started and fruitfully investigate the interactions among globalization, culture and society in ethnic Mongolia. I hope that if my preceding remarks have accomplished anything, they will convince our readers that our area of inquiry, largely ignored until now, offers a vast range of research options. It would indeed be foolish of me to try to list more than a handful here.

Keeping in mind the three areas mentioned at the start of my remarks -- the spatial comparison of Northern and Southern Mongolia, the temporal comparison between the present situation and that during the Mongol world empire, and the special China factor -- here are some possible targets for future investigations. What changes in which aspect of Mongolian culture and society have taken place during the last decade, and in what ways are those changes related to the process of globalization? Have these changes been the same or similar in both northern and southern

---

[19] A term originating in technology where it means the ability to transfer data back and forth among various devices.

Mongolia? If they are different, to what factors may the differences be attributed? Turning the argument around, we should also ask whether Mongolian culture has in any way shaped the nature and/or intensity of globalization within ethnic Mongolia? When comparing different historical periods, we may ask how, if at all, globalization affected which aspects of Mongolian culture and society then, as compared with its effects on contemporary Mongolia? Conversely, what comparisons might we draw between the impact of Mongolian culture on globalization during these two periods in Mongolian history? And finally, when we look at the huge changes in China's relationship with Mongolia between then and now, should we simply explain them in terms of relative military and political strength, or have other forces been at work as well?

The Mongolian Ideology of Tenggerism and Khubilai Khan

Shagdaryn Bira

It was a belief in the Tenggeri (Heaven-God) that inspired and motivated the unprecedented rise of the Mongols in the thirteenth and fourteenth centuries, and this belief was eventually developed to the point that it constituted a cohesive political theory that can be called Tenggerism or Heavenism.

The ideology of Tenggerism went through three stages of development. It first emerged during the period when Chinggis Khan founded the Great Mongol State in 1206. At that time it was aimed at the sacralization and legitimization of the power of his Eurasian nomadic empire. The second stage occurred during the period of the world-wide expansionism of Chinggis Khan's successors. At that time Tenggerism developed into a sophisticated universal ideology of Tenggerization, according to which all under Heaven must be united under the rule of the Mongols. The third stage of Tenggerism commenced with the reign of Khubilai Khan, who completed the creation of the universal empire by conquering the whole of China. Unlike his predecessors, Khubilai Khan was less concerned with conquests than with the problems of pacifying and consolidating the universal empire.

I have already dealt with the first two stages of this process in some of my previous writings.[1] At this time I would like to speak about the third stage. It was during Khubilai Khan's thirty-five

---

1 Sh. Bira, "Mongolian Tenggerism and Modern Globalism: A Retrospective Outlook on Globalism," *Journal of the Royal Asiatic Society* 14 (2004), 3-12.

years of rule that the Mongolian policy of Tenggerization reached its apogee and the Mongolian empire acquired its universal character. The world was actually united under one political authority. It was interconnected by the communication network known as the *örtöge* system of horse relay stations. Peoples, ideas, information, and commerce flowed freely between countries through this network. Examples include the creation and introduction of an international alphabet, the so-called square script, which encouraged the cultural integration of many ethnic groups and the construction of an astronomical observatory at Maraghah in Azerbaijan. The famous observatory was headed by the great astronomer Nasir ad-Din at-Tusi (1201-1274). It became a meeting place of scientists from various countries and there developed a close collaboration between Arab-Iranian and Chinese astronomers. In 1267 Khubilai Khan invited the Iranian astronomer Jamal ad-Din to his capital Dadu, the present-day Beijing. The astronomer brought the astronomical instruments sent by Il-Khan Hülegü to his brother Khubilai Khan. The famous Chinese astronomer Guo Shoujing (1231-1316) together with his Iranian colleague Jamal ad-Din founded an observatory in the capital of the empire, and their research was most fruitful.

It was during the Mongol Yüan dynasty that the Mongols came into direct contact with a variety of cultures, including Chinese, Indo-Tibetan, Arab-Islamic and Central Asian. Buddhist literature was translated from different languages into Mongolian. Not a few Mongols mastered the Chinese language and script. They took an active part in literary and translation activities, and some of them even wrote their works in Chinese. Uighurs, Tanguts, Tibetans, Chinese and Central Asians worked in close collaboration with Mongols. In 1307 Bolodtemür, the Assistant of the Left in the Secretarial Council, presented to Qaisan Khan a Mongolian version of the famous Confucian book *Xiaojing* in the so-called state script. The Mongols also became acquainted with the stories of the famous Alexander Romance. Möngke Khan's minister Mahmud Yalavach once related to his sovereign a story from the Muslim version of the Alexander Romance, and the Mongol khan was extremely pleased with it. The Alexander Romance soon gained wider popularity and in the early fourteenth century the entire work is said to have been translated into Mongolian.

The exchange of intellectual achievements across the Eurasian continent found its most illustrious expression in the world's first universal history known as *Jami'al-Tawarikh* ("The Compendium of Histories"), compiled by Rashid ad-Din with the assistance and participation of an international team of historians, including the Mongol Bolod (Pulad) chingsiang. The close collaboration and friendship of Rashid ad-Din and Bolod chingsiang are very symbolic in terms of cultural rapprochement between East and West. Thomas Allsen writes that "when acknowledged at all, our Bolod is usually described, quite accurately, as a literate Mongolian and as the informant of Rashid al-Din. But he was much more than that. He may be justly characterized as a Mongolian intellectual-literate, cosmopolitan, and a man of affairs. Although continuously exposed to foreign cultures and to their leading representatives, he never abandons his ties to Mongolian traditions. Bolod, of course, knew much about Chinese and later Persian culture, but he remained to his dying day 'the expert' on Mongolian customs and genealogy."[2]

I have given some details only from the intellectual sphere. More details can be gleaned from the economic, commercial and humanitarian interconnections in those days. All of these facts show that there had been developing something more than military conquests of nomadic "barbarians" who brought nothing but destruction and massacre. Rather there took place some kinds of global processes that, in some ways, can be compared with modern globalization, specially in terms of making peoples and countries closer and more integrated than ever before.

Khubilai Khan was a great reformer of the Mongolian ideology of world domination. He knew his own nomadic civilization as well as the Confucian, Buddhist, Arab-Islamic and European-Christian civilizations, and he did his utmost to exploit their gains successfully and selectively in conformity with his policy of Tenggerization. He explained his religious policy to Marco Polo as

---

[2] Thomas T. Allsen, *Culture and Conquest in Mongol Eurasia* (Cambridge: Cambridge University Press, 2002), 79-80.

follows: ”There are four gods worshipped by everybody. Jesus Christ of the Christians, Mohammed of the Iranians, Moses of the Jews and Buddha Chandamani. As regards myself, I respect all of those four religions, but whosoever is the greatest and most honest in heaven, I wish to have bless me”.[3]

History confirms that the Mongolian khan finally gave preference to Buddhism as a neutral and more universal religion in comparison with other religions known to him. His political pragmatism allowed him to find the universal and supranational character of Buddhism well suited to the model of his multinational universal emperorship. As is well-known, since ancient times Buddhism had been developing an original ideology in which the chakravartin-rāja concept occupied center stage. According to this ideology the world should be united under the banner of Buddhism and ruled by universal monarchs who turn the wheel of Dhārma. It should be pointed out that in the pro-Buddhist policy of Khubilai Khan the most decisive role was played by hPhags-pa Lama, the famous abbot of the Sa-skya monastery of Tibet. The fact that Khubilai's policy towards Buddhist Tibet differed greatly from that towards other countries essentially reflected his specific attitude to Buddhism. Tibet, as a matter of fact, was not conquered by force, but joined to the Mongol empire by way of establishing a predominantly spiritual relationship called by the Tibetans themselves a Yong-mchod (Yong-bdag-mchod gna, in Mongolian: ögli-ge-yin ejen, takil-un orun) or "Alms-giver-Religious Preceptor" relationship which eventually expressed the sacred meaning of the union of the so-called two orders, that of the Union of the Khan or "Alms-giver" as the head of the secular power and the Preceptor as the head of the ecclesiastic power.

In reality, however, the Yong-mchod relationship was not an equal partnership of the two heads of power. The khan as "the Alms-giver" played the leading role and provided the Preceptor with donations, while the Preceptor as the spiritual leader served to sanctify and legitimate the khan's power. One can say that this was the Mongolian interpretation and modification of the old traditional Indo-Tibetan conception of the Buddhist monarchy on

---

3 A.C. Moulle, *Marco Polo* (Cambridge: Cambridge University Press, 1957), 201.

the basis of the Mongolian ideology of Tenggerism. After acute disputes at their first meeting, Khubilai Khan and hPhags-pa Lama reached a concordance according to which the oldest Buddhist doctrine of unity of the ecclesiastical and temporal orders underwent a major transformation. Khubilai Khan saw to it that the traditional hegemony of the Buddhist religion over the state power was going to be limited, while hPhags-pa Lama succeeded in getting a special status for his country as a spiritual center of the Mongolian empire. Tibet of that period reminds us to a certain extent of the Vatican in the modern age.

Khubilai Khan carried out bold reforms in the universal ideology of his predecessors. Not rejecting Shamanism and its ideology, he preferred to apply the main tenets of Buddhist universalism to his policy of Tenggerization. By the Order of Khubilai Khan issued on the first day of the middle summer month of the Year of the Mouse (1264) and called the hjah-sa mo-tig-ma ("The Pearl Yasa") the Mongol khan, although traditionally referring both to the power of everlasting Tenggeri[4] and protection of the khan's charisma (*suu jali*) in the beginning of his Order, stated as follows:

> "Though one should follow the law of Chinggis Khan to reach all the best in this life, it is necessary to rely upon the Law of Buddha after this life. Having perceived the meaning of all this [I] have understood the path of Shakyamuni as a genuine path only. It is my teacher hPhags-pa Lama who, having well understood himself that path, has well taught this path to others. This is why I have received the dbang (abisheka) from him and awarded him the title of guoshri (Chinese: guoshi), the State Preceptor, and he was declared to be venerated by all huvrags (lamas)..."[5]

---

[4] "I have reconstructed the Mongolian original from the Tibetan: tse-ring gnam-gyi..."

[5] See my *O "Zolotoi knige" Sh. Damdina* (Ulaanbaatar : Izd-vo Akademii nauk MNR, 1964), 73-74. Cf. *Pagba lama-yin tuguji* (Kökeqota: Öbör Monggol-un Arad-un Keblel-ün Qoriy-a, 1992), 43-56.

In the same Order hPhags-pa Lama was designated as the Head of Religion, and all the huvraqs or lamas of Tibet were required to obey him and be engaged exclusively in religious services for the welfare of the Mongol khan according to the precepts of the Buddhist teaching. Under these conditions only the khan would indispensably provide the lamas with his donations and veneration, and would free them from "the three duties" - military service, taxes and örtöge duties.

This Order marked a turning point in the ideology of Khubilai Khan's Tenggerism. He actually declared Buddhism to be the state religion, having appointed hPhags-pa Lama the State Preceptor. At the same time he underlined his loyalty to the power of Tenggeri and the protection of the khan. Here one can see some kind of division of power with preference given to the khan's power. It is characteristic that almost all the edicts issued by Khubilai Khan's successors, like Buyantu Khan, and imperial family members, like Mangala, Dhārmapala's widow, Ananda consistently referred to the power or strength of Eternal Heaven and the khan's charisma (*suu*), thus demonstrating their loyalty to their traditional ideology of Tenggerism. Although these documents dealt with the affairs of different religions -- Buddhism, Christianity, Taoism, and Islam -- their representatives were ordered to pray to Heaven and pronounce benedictions in favor of the Mongol khans.[6]

It is obvious from the Order and other, similar sources that Mongolian Tenggerism did not clash with Buddhist universalism, as it did with Islam and Christianity during the reigns of Khubilai Khan's predecessors. Moreover, Tenggerism was being considerably transformed under the impact of the fundamental ideological principles of Buddhism. Source materials, particularly Tibetan, testify that with the active participation and assistance of hPhags-pa Lama the Mongol khan managed to put Buddhism into the service of his universal emperorship. Thus a new philosophy arose with the aim of supporting and justifying the policy of Tenggerization of the Mongols.

---

[6] Nicholas Poppe, *The Mongolian Monuments in hPhags-pa Script* (Wiesbaden: Otto Harrassowitz, 1957), 46-56.

By his numerous works, especially those addressing Khubilai Khan and his family members, hPhags-pa Lama did much to substantiate the universal nature of the Mongol empire and legitimate the right of the Mongol ruler as the Chakravartin-rāja. In his well-known work *Shes-bya rab-gsal* (The Book to Clarify Knowledge), hPhags-pa Lama did his best to justify the universal character of the Mongol empire from the viewpoint of Buddhist historiography. The book was composed by order of Khubilai Khan's son, Crown Prince Chingim, in the Year of the Earth Tiger (1278). The State Preceptor was the first to include the Mongol empire in the scheme of the general history of the Buddhist world and to call Chinggis Khan a Chakravartin khan (in Tibetan: hkor los sgyur-'ba'i rgyalbo).

This was quite a new initiative in the Buddhist historiography of that time. The author gave a brief survey of the Mongol empire just after the history of ancient India and Tibet, the two great Buddhist countries. Hence there first appeared, as I have written previously, a three Buddhist monarchy scheme (India, Tibet, and Mongolia) of writing history in Tibetan and Mongolian historical writings. According to this scheme the history of the Mongol empire was incorporated into the history of the Buddhist universe, and Chinggis Khan and his successors were linked to the sacred genealogies of the great Buddhist kings of India and Tibet, beginning with Mahāsammata, the legendary forefather of all the kings of the Buddhist world.

I want to emphasize that hPhags-ps Lama did not falsify history by forcefully linking the genealogical bloodlines of the great Mongol khans with those of the ancient Indian and Tibetan Dhārma-rājas, as Mongol historians did later on. He only confirmed that there was a universal empire founded by Chinggis Khan, and that this empire became a Buddhist one under the rule of Khubilai Khan. On this basis, he had some reason for including the Mongol empire into the list of Buddhist countries and for comparing Chinggis Khan with Chakravartin and likening Khubilai Khan to the Bodhisattva, calling him a Dhārma-rāja, the supporter and protector of the all-victorious Buddhist teaching. One year before Khubilai became khan, hPhags-pa Lama elevated him to the level of a great Boddhisattva khan and wished many blessings on him.[7] In one of his blessings he called Khubilai "the highest Boddhisattva, friend of the Dhārma, the right and merciful protector of the world".[8]

In another blessing hPhags-pa Lama praised Khubilai Khan as the highest Boddhisattva Sechen Khan, distinguished by his virtues, prominent for his sincere belief and merciful wisdom, the advocate of religion and the protector of the world by his honest mind".[9] The elevation of the Mongol khan as a Boddhisattva by the head of a religion pursued, after all, a far-reaching aim. According to the Buddhist worldview, the Boddhisattva ideal of the king represented a cosmic liberation that not only delivers his subjects from all miseries, but provides a cosmic unity, integration and harmony to the Universe. And it is not difficult for us to imagine that Khubilai Khan was not only extremely flattered by all this praise, but he accepted it as objectively correct because the khan had, after all, been tireless in his attempts to unite "all under Heaven" by all possible means.

Khubilai Khan's new approach towards the policy of Tenggerization found its most impressive reflection in the fact that he himself converted to Buddhism by way of receiving a consecration (abisheka, Tibetan: dbang) from hPhags-pa Lama, and the act of consecration was repeated for three times. The first time was in 1253, when he was not yet a khan but involved in Tibetan affairs, and the two others occurred in 1260 and 1270. The abisheka which he received was that of Hevajra (Tibetan: dges-pa rdorje), the Tantric deity (yi-dam). Hevajra is one of the main tutelary deities in Lamaism who was especially worshipped in the Sa-skya monasteries and whose cult is closely linked with that of Mahākāla (Tibetan: mGon-po). hPhags-pa Lama himself is believed to have received the initiation in Hevajra by Mahākāla.

---

7 hPhags-pa bla-ma, rGyal-po la gdams-pa'i rab-du byed-pa (Sa-skya bkah-hbum), Vol. Ba, ff. 1a/344-37a/430a.

8 Sa-skya bkah-hbum, Vol. Va, ff. 3a/390b

9 *Pagba lama-yin tuguji*, Coyiji, ed. (Kökeqota: Öbör Monggol-un Arad-un Keblel-ün Qoriy-a, 1992), 53.

The fact that Khubilai Khan got the initiation in Hevajra rites from the direct transmitter had, from the point of view of Tantrism, a great magic meaning in terms of enhancing his God-like nature and legitimating his universal khanship. By having gotten into direct spiritual contact with his tutelary deity Mahākāla, the most powerful defender of religion, Khubilai Khan could claim to have acquired all his mysterious powers in the cause of ruling his empire. Thus, the Mongolian khanship could enjoy not only the

Mahākāla

favor of Tenggri, but the favor of the powerful Tantric god. The black figure of terrifying Mahākāla had actually become a symbol of the khan's might just as the Shamanist black *sülde* had been the symbol of Chinggis Khan's power.

In 1270 on the initiatives of Khubilai Khan and hPhags-pa Lama there was built a temple consecrated to Mahākāla in the place of Zhuozhou located south of Dadu. At the temple there used to take place great rituals dedicated to Mahākāla, the fearful defender who suppressed all evil forces of state and religion. These rituals were held especially frequently during times of war. The cult of Mahākāla continued until the end of the Yüan dynasty, and many temples dedicated Mahākāla were constructed in different parts of China. Even though they were no longer held after the fall of the Yuan dynasty, these rituals created a tradition of Mahākāla worship among the Mongols that continued until modern times. Tankas and statuettes of Mahākāla had been kept in most Mongolian families including my own, as he came to be widely regarded as the main defender and protector of the Mongolian nation.

Judging by the description by Chos-kyi-'od-zer (fl. 1305-1321) in his poem devoted to Mahākāla ("The Great Black"), the deity was represented in those days as being of black color, having a terrifying image with four hands, one face, three red eyes symbolizing the past, present, and future, and yellow hair, and holding a sword in his front right hand, a scull in the other right hand, a spear in his upper left hand, and the dvaja or victory banner in his lower left hand. This description largely corresponds to the terrifying form of Siva in her character as destroyer. Siva is one member of the Hindu triad of deities, the two other being Brahma "the creator" and Vishnu "the preserver". This close similarity means that the worship of Mahākāla was traditionally associated with that of Siva, who was also depicted in the black color as Mahākāla.

The other tutelary deity whom Khubilai Khan had chosen was Sitātapatra, in Mongolian Čagan Sikürtei and in Tibetan gdugs-dkar čan. In 1270 Khubilai Khan, on the advice of hPhags-pa Lama, hoisted over his throne in the Da Ming Palace in Dadu the white parasol of the Tantric god Sitātapatra. With that act Khubilai Khan turned the Tantric deity into the protector of the Mongol empire. As is known, the white parasol was popular in Buddhist countries as an emblem of royalty signifying peace and prosperity, and Khubilai Khan used it alongside the white *sülde* or banner of Chinggis Khan as the "sülde of peace". The white color and the calm, peaceful image of Sitātapatra probably resonated well with the Mongols of Khubilai Khan's days as they soon began to identify the Tantric deity with their own shamanistic "protective spirit", the *čagan tug*, which was the white standard first raised by Chinggis Khan as a symbol of peace and protection at the ceremony of his enthronement in 1206.

Sitātapatra

One should point out that the ideological and practical meaning of the worship of the Tantric deity Sitātapatra was far-reaching in terms of sacralizing and pacifying the world empire of the Mongol khans. Whoever worshipped this deity (*yi-dam*) entered into a mysterious and intimate union with his tutelary spirit and enjoyed her peaceful magic powers and favors. Although Tantrism was introduced into the Mongolian empire from Tibet, its origin goes back to the ancient Indian worship of the feminine as a prime cause of all phenomena. Therefore, in Tantrism most deities (yi-dam) are depicted as feminine. The yi-dam Sitātapatra is traditionally represented as a female deity with all her attributes. Her color is pure white with many hands and faces, keeping a vajra in her main right hand and the white parasol with the long handle in her main left hand, suppressing innumerable evil forces under her big waist band. One can find images of Sitātapatra as described here in the illustrations of the Mongolian version of the Kanjur.[10]

Researchers like Herbert Franke and Choyiji have produced some interesting data from the *Yuan shi* concerning the rituals of Sitātapatra that had been suggested by hPhags-pa Lama and introduced at the imperial court by Khubilai Khan. The rituals of Sitātapatra were held every year on the fifteenth day of the middle month of spring, beginning in the year 1270. During the colorful ceremony, participated in by the khan and the state preceptor and a large number of dignitaries, the white parasol was taken from the khan's palace and carried in the procession circumambulating the capital city. The ceremony was attended by huge crowds of people and looked in all respects like a great festival that included both religious and cultural forms of colorful entertainment. After the end of the procession the white parasol was returned to the imperial palace and again hoisted over the khan's throne.[11]

10Rasisereng, *Monggol "Ganjuur" daki Burqan-u burin iji körüg jirug : Degedu* (Kökeqota: Öbör Monggol-un Arad-un Keblel-ün Qoriy-a, 2002), 78.

11Herbert Franke, *From Tribal Chieftain to Universal Emperor and God: The Legitimation of the Yüan Dynasty* (München: Verlag der BAW, 1978), 60-62; Coyiji, *Monggol-un burqan-u sasin-u teüke: Yeke Monggol ulus-un üy-e, 1206-1271* (Kökeqota: Öbör Monggol-un Arad-un Keblel-ün Qoriy-a, 1998), 283-284.

The worship of Sitātapatra and the rituals associated with it were designed to demonstrate to the huge crowds attending the annual festivities and to the empire as a whole the khan's power to ensure peace and welfare for all. At the same time, the rituals served to demonstrate the god-like nature of the Mongol khans as Chakravartin emperors of the universe.

In conclusion, one should say that during the Yuan period of the Mongol empire the traditional Mongolian ideology of Tenggerism underwent great changes thanks to the impact of Buddhist religious and political philosophy. When compared with other religions and ideologies known to the Mongol khans at the time, Buddhism offered them a form of universalism that, thanks to its supranational and cosmopolitan nature, was far more attuned to the needs of governing a world empire. Rather than replacing Tenggerism, the Buddhist model of the monarch as Chakravartin strengthened it by serving as a new innovative paradigm for imitation, invocation and, finally, for deification of the Mongolian khans in their attempts to justify and legitimatize their world domination.

The Mongol Yuan dynasty represented in its ideology and form more of a Buddhist universal monarchy than the Chinese or nomadic types of Eastern empires. The introduction by Khubilai Khan, on hPhags-pa Lama's initiative, of an elaborate court cult and colorful ceremonies of Indo-Tibetan Buddhist Tantric deities, particularly Mahākāla and Sitātapatra, was bound to demonstrate the Buddhist god-like nature of the universal khanship. If Tenggerism justified the world-wide conquests of the Mongols, Buddhism in the form of Tibetan Lamaism was worshiped with the aim of sacralizing the peaceful domination of the numerically small elite of Mongols over all the world.

BIBLIOGRAPHY

Allsen, Thomas T. *Culture and Conquest in Mongol Eurasia.* Cambridge: Cambridge University Press, 2002.

Bira, Shagdaryn. "Mongolian Tenggerism and Modern Globalism: A Retrospective Outlook on Globalism," *Journal of the Royal As-*

iatic Society 14 (2004), 3-12.

Coyiji. *Monggol-un burqan-u sasin-u teüke: Yeke Monggol ulus-un üy-e, 1206-1271*. Kökeqota: Öbör Monggol-un Arad-un Keblel-ün Qoriy-a, 1998.

Franke, Herbert. *From Tribal Chieftain to Universal Emperor and God: The Legitimation of the Yüan Dynasty*. München: Bayerische Akademie der Wissenschaften, 1978.

Moulle, A.C. *Marco Polo*. Cambridge: Cambridge University Press, 1957.

Pagba lama-yin tuguji. Kökeqota: Öbör Monggol-un Arad-un Keblel-ün Qoriy-a, 1992.

Poppe, Nicholas. *The Mongolian Monuments in hPhags-pa Script*. Wiesbaden: Otto Harrassowitz, 1957.

Rasisereng. *Monggol "Ganjuur" daki Burqan-u burin iji körüg jirug : Degedu*. Kökeqota: Öbör Monggol-un Arad-un Keblel-ün Qoriy-a, 2002.

Globalization and Mongolia: Blessing or Curse?[1]

Paul D. Buell and Ngan Le

> "After us the descendants of our clan will wear gold embroidered garments, eat rich and sweet food, ride fine horses, and embrace beautiful women but they will not say that they owe all this to their fathers and elder brothers, and they will forget us and those great times."
>
> "Whoever can clean his own house can rid the country of thieves."
>
> Sayings of Činggis-qan (Riasanovsky, 1965: 88, 89)

Since 1991, Mongolia, no longer part of the Soviet command economy, has been in the process of adapting to the demands of a new world economic system. It is now required to sink or swim based on the dictates of a distant marketplace that has very little to do with conditions in Mongolia itself. It has been able to cope only to a most limited degree and today Mongolia survives largely from handouts from international organizations and donor countries. As has been the case in many other parts of the world, the demands of globalization have dislocated Mongolian society at its very roots. In the pages that follow, we will look at one key area of this dislocated society, Mongolia's pastoral sector. There privatization, a key goal of Mongolia's economic modernization as dictated

[1] We would like to thank Morris Rossabi and Gene Anderson for taking the time to read over and criticize our paper. Their help and encouragement were invaluable.

by its creditors, has undermined not only pastoral production itself, but Mongolia's whole traditional way of life in the process. Among the casualties has been Mongolia's ability to feed its people. Pastoralism remains its primary native source of food and has remained so for centuries. Given its other needs, imported petroleum and petroleum products,[2] for example, and a high debt load, Mongolia lacks the wherewithal to import enough food to feed its growing population adequately. In addition to the products of its pastoralism, Mongolia does produce other kinds of foods, principally grain, potatoes, and hardy vegetables, but supplies are in no way sufficient to need and privatization has had a highly negative impact on Mongolia's grain and vegetable agriculture as well as on its pastoralism. What is available from local production is, in most cases, very expensive. Only in the products of pastoralism, dairy products and meat, the source of cheap food for the vast majority of the population, is Mongolia fully self-sufficient, although distribution problems often limit availability and production is becoming more and more inefficient. All other food products, beyond the little grain and vegetables produced locally, and small amounts of game meats and traditional gathered plant foods, must be imported and once Mongolia has paid for its oil and industrial goods, and has serviced its debts, not much foreign exchange to meet a growing food deficit remains. Hunger and mal-nourishment, rarely the case before, are now real threats.

---

[2] In 2003, the last year for which full figures are available Mongolia imported 512,900 tons of petroleum products, including 259,100 tons of gasoline and 214,800 tons of Diesel fuel, and had a trade deficit of 185.1 million US dollars (*Statisikiyn Emkhtegel*, 2004), largely due to its petroleum imports. By contrast, Mongolia exported, to China, 159,900 barrels of oil to China from its own oilfields located in the wrong part of Mongolia to contribute to national needs. Although an increasing amount of Mongolia's gasoline is processed in its own refineries, to save money, its dependence upon foreign petroleum remains large and its financial burden from this source has grown greatly with the major price increases of recent years. Only further development of Mongolia's own oil is likely to change this situation and this will have to wait not only increased exploration and development, but considerable investment in local and national infrastructure to bring domestic oil to the domestic market. Thus Mongolia's position as a net oil importer is unlikely to change any time in the near future. Most of Mongolia's oil now comes from Kazakhstan (*Jane's Sentinel*, 2004).

Despite its participation in the new world economy of globalization, Mongolia thus remains heavily reliant upon the declining output of its traditional, pastoral sector as its primary food source. It has no other choice but the sector is in serious trouble and as hunger grows in Mongolia there is increasing social dislocation. The reasons for this are many. Key are organizational changes, namely the collapse of much of Mongolia's rural infrastructure, and changing herding practices brought about as a consequence of organizational breakdowns and the associated privatization of livestock since the end of Mongolia's Soviet period. At another level, greater forces are at work, running the gamut of all on-going social change in Mongolia. Mongolia, for example, is squandering its traditional social capital, the glue that has held Mongolian society together for centuries.

Social capital may be defined in various ways (Sobel, 2002). The World Bank (PovertyNet: "Social Capital") defines it the "norms and networks that enable collective action," a definition that works very well for Mongolia. There the term above all refers to the traditional collective institutions and associated social laws and mores that keep Mongolian society functioning. It also implies certain traditional resources, such as traditional knowledge systems and human resources. This includes the traditional leadership of pastoral society, those individuals who know how to make pastoralism work best in difficult and environmentally sensitive areas, the case virtually everywhere in Mongolia.

Mongolian pastoralism continues to embrace more of the territory of Mongolia than any other economic activity. It clearly involves much more than simply having a few animals, pasturing them as needed, and getting them to market, however possible. Good pastoralists must know exactly how to raise their animals, exactly how and where to pasture them, when to move them, and, most importantly, how to keep them alive or with minimal losses through the winter. Mongolian pastoralism also involves a sophisticated understanding of the environment, in terms of its direct uses for pastoralism and in terms of other possibilities that it offers for survival beyond pastoralism. The good pastoralist, for example, must know how to gather plant foods when pastoral products are in short supply, or how and what to hunt. To accomplish these things, the good pastoralist must know how to utilize social institutions, his social capital, to his own benefit. He needs systems of mutual support and cooperative institutions to coordinate pastoral activities. This is a vital function in an unforgiving landscape (Fernandez-Giménez, 1999; Sneath, 1999; 2002; Sheehy, 1999; Humphrey and Sneath, 1996; Telenged, 1996). It may or may not take a village to raise a child, but it certainly takes a whole network to raise livestock in the Mongolian steppe.

Once its traditional social capital, above all its truly capable herdsmen working together as part of formal institutional networks, and all the traditional knowledge and systems associated with them, is gone, Mongolia could face starvation; at the least an unacceptable level of adverse social and cultural change. Today the brightest and the best are steadily fleeing the pastoral life,[3] meaning growing future difficulties in sustaining it. Larger movements, which have already begun to take place with the worsening of conditions, could spell national catastrophe. If Mongolia's pastoral population as a whole, or most of it, moves into the cities, not only will the pastoral sector itself collapse but with it Mongolian society as a whole. An Ulaanbaatar of two or more millions, twice the present population, mostly poor people, with a few sheep and other livestock, right in town, and living in smoky yurts[4] without plumbing or other amenities would mean disaster by any measure. Ulaanbaatar is barely able to sustain its present overflow, much less twice as many.[5] And how can such an overflow exist solely on

[3] This is particularly true for the better educated population of the Mongolian middle administrative units, the *somon*, formerly the principal service centers supporting pastoralism locally. Some 77 percent are now in danger of disappearing and within them virtually all social and other services to the pastoral sector (*EDN*, 15 November 2002; 3 December 2002).

[4] According to an estimate published by the Mongolian newspaper *Unen*, some 140,000 families in the Ulaanbaatar *ger* or yurt district used wood and coal for heating in early 2003, often in inefficient hand-made stoves. Some 140,000 tons of wood and 600,000 tons of coal were then being consumed. Demand is likely to have risen since. Also contributing to Ulaanbaatar air pollution, among the worst in the world, are the city's coal-fired power plants, the source of 60 percent of its air pollution (*EDN*, 6 January 2003).

[5] The official population of Ulaanbaatar is projected to reach 919,000 by 2010 at present growth rates. Official estimates were 821,800 at the end of 2002, up 3.9 percent over the previous year, and 854,200 at the end of 2003. Some 23,778 officially migrated in 2003, with the total population growth of the capital amounting to 25.8 percent between 1995 and 2001. None of the current off-

imported food given that Mongolia is unlikely to develop economically fast enough for it to obtain the required foreign exchange (most of Mongolia's trading partners are unwilling to take tugriks) to feed a loose population in the millions?

Below we look carefully first at Mongolia's traditional pastoralism, as it has developed over the centuries, in the more than 800 years since the Mongols first achieved nationhood, and at its distant Eurasian roots. Particular attention will be paid to pastoralism as a strategy for producing food and as a social system to apply Mongolian social capital to producing food. Next, we will look at the threats that exist to the pastoral way of life today and the ways in which it is changing, adversely, in response to these threats. In the end, if globalization is going to be of much benefit to Mongolia, it must not be at the expense of its traditional way of life that still employs a majority of Mongols and it must not destroy Mongolia's food production base in the process. To be sure, a new Mongolia, one based in mineral extraction and industrialization, with better infrastructure, the current focus of foreign aid, is em-

icial population figures takes into account the floating population estimated at between 70,000, a low estimate, and 200,000. Nearly a third of Ulaanbaatar's population is comprised of children under 16 and there are large numbers of street children, at least 3500 of them in 2001, and other derelicts living in the sewer system, at least some 10,000 homeless people in all. Some 70 percent of the total population lives in the city's *ger* districts, which lack rudiments such as running water and sewage systems and where most of the available electricity there is illegally tapped. It is estimated that 27-38 percent of the capital's able-bodied population lacks permanent employment. Although Ulaanbaatar now accounts for only about one-third of Mongolia's total population, it accounted for 47.5 percent of all Mongolian crime in 2002, pointing up the social problems of the capital (*EDN*, 9 April 2001; 28 March 2001; 13 December 2002; 8 January 2003; 20 January 2003; 9 April 2003; 12 December 2003; *UBPost*, 6 December 2004). Ulaanbaatar is Mongolia's largest market for food products. In 2002, its population consumed 98.2 kg of meat per capita, along with 51.2 kg of milk and dairy products, some 138.3 kg of flour, 0.5 kg of butter and oil, 21.2 kg of granulated sugar, 38.7 kg of potatoes, 17 kg of vegetables, 0.5 kg of fish, 17.1 kg of rice, 12.8 kg of fruits and berries, 24.1 kg of eggs, and 9 kg of vegetable oil (*EDN*, 16 May 2002). According to another estimate, Ulaanbaatar in mid-2002 had an annual requirement of 59,000 tons of meat and meat products, 147,800 tons of dairy products, 5.1 thousand tons of cream, and 70,900 eggs. By 2010 the figures are expected to be 82,800 tons of meat, 175,500 tons of milk, 52,200 tons of flour. Altogether, demand was expected to increase 1.2 times by 2005 and 1.5 times by 2010 (*EDN*, 9 April 2001; 31 July 2002).

erging. But this new Mongolia will need substantial help from abroad, help often with strings attached, for decades to come, just to function. There is the question as to whether or not this new Mongolia will come into being fast enough to offset the losses of production and social capital in the pastoral sector. Mongolia will remain dependent on it for the foreseeable future if its people are going to eat and if a growing population is going to find adequate employment. We conclude that perhaps another approach will be needed, one protecting the old Mongolia while the new develops.

THE MONGOLIAN BACKDROP

Mongolia is a large country (1,565,000 km^2 or about a fifth the size of the United States), with a relatively small population estimated by the *CIA World Factbook* at 2,791,292 in July 2005. This is about 1.78 persons per km^2. The population is predominately young, with a median age estimated at 24.28 in 2005 and is growing at an estimated rate of 1.45 percent per annum. This is a considerable drop over earlier years. Literacy is high, nearly 98 percent in 2002 (*CIA World Factbook*), although, given the collapse of much of Mongolia's social infrastructure, including education, there is probably reason to doubt this figure and it has almost certainly fallen since. There are substantial mineral resources of every kind, most importantly copper and gold but also some petroleum, but Mongolia's infrastructure, particularly its transportation system, is too underdeveloped to maximize profitability. Mongolia's principal trading partners are Russia and China, with the United States an increasingly important economic participant, taking 23.2 percent of Mongolia's exports in 2003 although contributing few of Mongolia's imports in that year, only 2.9 percent (*Statistikiin Emkhtgel* 2003). The country remains relatively poor with a GDP of an estimated $5.332 billion in 2004, about $1,900 per capita (*CIA World Factbook*).[6] Mongolia has one of the highest debt bur-

[6] Year 2004 GDP was said to be an increase of 10.6 percent over 2003 when GDP was up 5.5 percent over the previous year (Mongolia, Mineral Resources and Petroleum Authority, 2005). Internal estimates of per capital GDP tend to be considerably lower and are calculated on a different basis. See, for example, *EDN*, 30 December 2002.

den ratios in the world.[7] The country requires a steady flow of loans and subsidies to survive as a nation, although much of this is being invested productively (*Jane's Sentinel*, 2004). The most significant is infrastructure development, for example, including the Millennium Road Project (*Jane's Sentinel*, 2004), to drastically improve a transportation system that has been good only around the capital, with a northern connection to Russia and a southern one to China, and in a few other favored areas.

A large part of Mongolia's population, about 42% in 2003 (*CIA World Factbook*), is directly involved in pastoralism to some degree or another, and thus full time in some form of food production.[8] Mongolia's pastoralism has its roots in the distant past and has been the subject of much study pointing up the considerable variety of the activities involved (Buell, Anderson, and Perry, 2000; Bold, 2001). In general terms, for much of the last 3000 years almost the entire steppe zone of Eurasia, not just a few limited parts of it as today, was occupied by pastoral nomads. They lived in a world apart, by their own rules, and according to their own principles. Only the coming of the railways in the nineteenth century definitively altered this fact by making an effective military conquest and foreign occupation possible for the first time, and

---

[7] In 2001, Mongolia's foreign debt equaled 90 percent of its GDP (*EDN*, 8 February 2002).

[8] At the end of 2003, Mongolia had 25,427,700 head of livestock, up somewhat over 2002, with a total decline of more than 8 million head since 1999, the high water mark of Mongolia's capitalist pastoralism. There were, by contrast, 25.8 million head in 1990, at the beginning of Mongolia's transition to the market place. At the end of 2003 the Mongolian annual animal census showed 1,968,900 horses, 10,756,400 sheep, 10,652,900 goats, 1,792,800 cattle and 256,700 camels. Animals added during the year were 7,885,500, an increase which must be set against any losses and animals slaughtered, 3,707,400 in 2003, down sharply from previous years, including 8,119,300 in 2000 (*Statistikiin Emkhtgel*, 2003). This decline indicates that Mongolian herds are being sustained only with difficulty and that too many animals may have been slaughtered in the past to maintain herd viability, currently a major area of economic difficulty in Mongolia. Under normal conditions, some 6.5 to 7.5 million animals are consumed each year, more if meat exports rise (*EDN*, 3 January 2002; 2 January 2003; 7 January 2003; 4 March 2003; 13 March 2003; 7 November 2003). At the end of 2002 there were 243,200 families with animals of some kind, include 175,900 herdsman families, down somewhat over previous years, including 398,800 total herdsmen (*EDN*, 29 May 2003).

bringing with it a mass migration by sedentary farmers in many areas. The surviving pastoral nomads were in many cases made sedentary, absorbed or driven back to a few refuges too dry or too cold to support regular agriculture.

Three key elements make the pastoral nomadic way of life possible, and in the past gave pastoral societies the power to dominate other, sedentary societies located in their proximity.[9] First is the availability of horses in quality and quantity. The horse has been and remains the centerpiece of steppe life, culturally and economically. It is what makes both the mobility and extensive herding of the steppe nomad possible. In a few drier areas it has been supplemented, but rarely completely replaced, by the camel.

Second have been the herd animals that provide the primary livelihood of the nomad. Most important is the sheep. Today's steppe sheep is relatively small and generally has a poor quality wool, adequate for felt-making but usually not of much use for weaving, for which the nomad rarely has the time or interest to pursue. It has primarily been bred, like other steppe herd animals, for its ability to withstand difficult conditions. The open steppe is fiercely hot in the summer and cold in the winter, and the only regularly available fodder is often scanty natural pasture.

Less numerous, but scarcely less important, has been the goat. It is a more aggressive user of pasture resources than the sheep, and thus a useful supplement to less hardy sheep under particularly difficult conditions. Cattle remain uncommon since they are more difficult to maintain, but they were very useful in traditional times, before the coming of the automobiles and trucks, used for the same purpose today. They were then the only means for drawing the wooden carts upon which the worldly possessions of the nomad would be assembled.

Third is the physical paraphernalia of pastoral nomadic life. They have been developed over long periods of time with the specific requirements of steppe life in mind. A major component is the traditional nomadic tent, or yurt. It is easily transportable and yet warm and sturdy, with a framework of open lattice work over which layers of felt are added, today topped by a water-proof canvas. Also important are well-adapted clothing, primarily of sheep-

---

[9] The following is based on Buell, 2004. See also the updated information in Buell, forthcoming.

skin, an efficient harness for horses and cattle, and a great variety of specialized equipment and tools such as the lasso pole, or *urga*, used by the Mongols to catch horses without having to bring them to the ground.

The pastoralism practiced by the Iranian, Turkic, Mongol, and other nomadic peoples once and presently inhabiting the steppe zone has primarily involved a system of annual movement between low-lying winter pastures and mountain summer pastures, with many local variations.[10] Movements are carefully staged and planned in advance. Variations have included movement along rivers, upstream in summer, downstream in winter, and in flat, purely steppe areas, in a broad circular movement. These movements are to prevent exhaustion of local fodder resources by remaining in any one general area too long, and also to take advantage of seasonal resources such as the rich grass that grows in the mountains during the summer.

Foods[11] have come primarily from animals herded. Some food may come from whatever else can be secured during the annual trek, as long as the additional activities involved are not prejudicial to herding. Trading is included, and formerly, in less settled times, raiding. Herd animals provide milk, milk products, and meat, although during much of the year they are simply too valuable to slaughter. They are used instead primarily for breeding. Not only do animals raised for such purposes provide more dairy products, but yield larger herds in the autumn and early winter. Large numbers of animals then mean security over the rest of the winter when herd losses can be quite severe. It also gives the nomad the ability to cull animals at his choice for meat, when other sources of food are becoming rarer during the winter, and to manage herds in response to specific winter conditions. The trick is to reach the spring with a herd that is not too large for existing fodder resources, but which is still large enough to start the cycle over again. Meat eating is thus not the *raison d'être* of nomadic life, but is rather part of a specific strategy for life. It is dairy products, available throughout much of the year, in fresh or preserved form,

---

[10] For Mongolia these have been classified in Erdenebaatar, 1996.

[11] The discussion here is primarily from Buell, Anderson and Perry, 2000; Buell, 1999; 2002; 2004. On the sacred biology of the Altaic world see also Roux, 1966.

that are actually the nomad's most important food source, and not meat. Excessive meat eating usually occurred in nomadic societies only in extended contact situations such as after conquests.

Living primarily on dairy products is not a problem for most Europeans, but is for steppe groups since almost all are unable to digest fresh milk. We assume that this was true in the past as well. Thus dairy products were most commonly consumed by the nomads in an easily assimilated fermented form.[12] This was so widely the practice, in fact, that it came to be considered a characteristic of the steppe world by sedentary societies. Some even borrowed some of their terminology for fermented milk products from the steppe. It is thus no accident that the English word yogurt is a loan word from Turkish.

Various forms of yogurt are eaten in the steppe world, including yogurt dried for preservation (modern Turkish *kurut*). Used to produce it is primarily sheep's or goat's milk, but also cow's milk when this uncommon food was available. Horse and camel milk is technically also available for this purpose, but the preferred application of these milks is to make kumiss (*airag*). This was the food with the highest prestige in early steppe societies and continues to be so today, albeit under somewhat changed circumstances since few nomads today are able to own the necessary number of mares to produce a steady supply. It takes about sixty mares, though fewer milk camels, to supply one individual with a steady supply of kumiss during the summer months. This was the only season when an excess of horse or camel milk was available for kumiss production. Thus only the rich could enjoy the food in abundance, although almost any could enjoy at least some, and the rich were obligated to share. Even the rich rarely, if ever, had enough camels to supply any significant quantity.

Kumiss is sufficiently alcoholic to intoxicate, but its limited availability discourages alcoholism from this source. Kumiss is made in a large kumiss-making bag hung near the doors of traditional yurts. Everyone entering was responsible for giving it a punch or shake to keep the fermentation going. Once made, kumiss can be clarified to produce "black" kumiss. This process conc-

[12] For an introduction see now Indra, 2003.

entrates the alcohol slightly by removing the particulate matter but does not in any sense distill.

Meat, when seasonably available or when a special occasion arises, is usually eaten fresh. It can also be dried, as the Mongols of the imperial period (the thirteenth and fourteenth centuries) did to make campaign rations (Middle Mongolian *ši'usu*). All parts of a slaughtered animal are consumed, except for the wool, the hooves, and excrement. The latter should be pressed out of the intestines so that they too can be used, as noted in one of the sayings of Činggis-qan. The preferred cooking method is boiling because it is believed to capture the animal's essence or soul. It also helps make limited supplies of meat go farther, and meets the needs of thirsty nomads living in dry environments. In the past, meat was also occasionally roasted, but this practice varied from group to group, and also dependent on the amount of available meat. Moreover, unlike broth, roasted meat is more difficult to divide evenly with among the members of a group. Kebabs, the name of which points to their Persian origin, were not known among the early Central Eurasian nomads who seem to have adopted them not until the Middle Ages.

In addition to providing meat, slaughtered animals also provide fat for cooking other foods, although frying has been uncommon. Not all Central Eurasian nomads have the fat-tailed sheep whose tail (and rump) fat has become a staple in many areas, both for use as a cooking fat and for enriching other foods. Popular among Turkic nomads to this day is the stuffing of intestines to make a large sausage. Fat (suet) and blood are essential ingredients. Special parts of the sheep or goat are considered delicacies and are reserved for special personages. Among some steppe cultures, for example, the eyes are given to a senior person participating in a feast. In the past, rules also governed reserving certain parts of a newly slaughtered animal or game for guests or even for a passer-by, a practice among the early Mongols.[13]

---

[13] "After that, when Dobun-mergen one day when to hunt on Toqocaq Rise, he encountered Uriangqadai people in the forest. They had killed a three-year-old deer and were cooking its ribs and intestines. When Dobun-mergen spoke he said: "Please give me [some meat] as the share of meat due another [*nökör sirolqa ke'ejü'ü*]." Taking [only] half a breast side of the meat with the lungs, and the hide, they gave all [the rest of the] three-year-old deer's meat to Dobun-

As with many other cultures, eating is a community activity among steppe groups and is governed by rules that are sometimes rather complex. Similarly complex rules have also governed hospitality since ancient times. Among the Kazakhs, the powerful used to take advantage of these rules in order to eat at the expense of well-off nomads who were obligated to provide free feasting. Listen to poor Kiregkeng's lament, as told by the traditional Kazakh poet Aq-Balkhi Korghanbay:

> Much wealth of fortunate Kiregkeng,
> just like a boundless lake.
> Just like at an inlet on a river's side,
> Our whole people has come out to drink.[14]

Supplementing milk products and meat from herd animals with many gathered plant foods has been the practice since ancient times, as the *Secret History of the Mongols*, the earliest Mongolian historical work, makes clear. It records how, when Činggis-qan and his brothers were abandoned in the steppe by their father's retainers after his death, they were nourished by their mother Hö'elün with despised wild plant foods:

> The Tayyici'ut elder and young brothers, set out on
> trek, leaving behind on the pasture grounds Hö'elün-
> üjin [Lady Hö'elün], the widow, and the little children,
> the mother and the children:
>
> Hö'elün-üjin, being born a wise woman,
> when she nourished her little children,
> attaching firmly her *boqta* [high Mongolian hat],
> tying up her robe tightly,
> she went running upstream and downstream the Onon,
> She went collecting the wild apples and the bird cherries,
> day and night she nourished their throats.

---

mergen" (Buell, Anderson and Perry, 2000: 31-32; text in Rachewiltz, 1972: 14-15).

[14] Tolybekov, 1971: 124.

Mother Üjin, born with courage,
when she nourished her children favored by ancestral power [*sutan*], taking cypress sticks,
she nourished them digging up garden burnet and cinquefoil roots.

Mother Üjin's
children, nourished with wild garlic and wild onions,
managed to grow up to become *qans*.
The children of the proper Üjin-mother,
nourished with scarlet lily [bulbs],
became wise, well-behaved children.

The beautiful Üjin's
proper children,
nourished with garlic chives and wild onions,
became ancestral figures with posterities [*qoyira'ut sayit*].
Ending their lives by becoming hero-ancestral figures [*eres sayit*],
Bold and brave ones they would seem to have been made.
Agreeing with one another to nourish their mother,
stationing their mother on the banks of the Onon,
making bent fish hooks together,
they went fishing with hooks for miserable fish.
Bending a fish hook from a needle,
they were fishing with hooks for *jebüge* and *qadara*.
Weaving together nets and weirs,
they were fishing out little fry.
But they nourished to satisfaction their mother.[15]

Although the text implies that such foods were eaten only under conditions of extreme hardship, recent ethnographic data suggest that this practice was actually much more common. The modern Mongols know and use for their food scores of wild cere-

---

[15] Buell, Anderson and Perry, 2000: 37-38. Text in Rachewiltz, 1972: 28-29. We are indebted to Igor de Rachewiltz for help in identifying the plants and animals mentioned (unpublished letter of 19 October, 1990).

als, fruits and berries, mushrooms, bulbs, nuts, tubers, roots, and greens (detailed in Buell, Anderson and Perry, 2000), but we know that this practice was already recorded by Herodotus in his account of the steppe peoples of his time and by many later observers as well. It seems to have been a characteristic of pastoral steppe life from the beginning. Moreover, some of the plant foods were gathered for their medicinal value as well.

Another major source of food for steppe nomads is game, although they cannot hunt as freely today as they once did. Observers of the early Mongols and of other steppe peoples repeatedly noted their great interest in hunting, and not just of large animals. Among those mentioned are deer, wild pigs, wild sheep, antelopes, wolves, foxes, hares, marmots, and even rats and mice. The list is by no means exhaustive and does not include the large number of fowl that Marco Polo mentioned as Mongol game. Some Mongol groups also fished, as did Činggis-qan and his brothers, in order to survive. Some steppe groups even made a specialty of fishing, a fact noticed by an early thirteenth-century Chinese observer, the Taoist Li Zhichang.

During the time of the Mongol empire most animals were taken individually when in season, but the Mongols also engaged in massive battue hunts. Several groups, cooperating as they did in herding, would move in from all sides, driving all animals before them to be hunted at close quarters in a closed area. As game became gradually scarcer, this practice was eventually ended.

Some animals have sacral character and have to be killed in special ways, although most were simply hunted with bow and arrow in the old days before guns. In recent times Kazakhs, for example, try not to shed the blood of wolves, but capture them in such a way that the animals break their own necks after being roped to a saddle of a moving horse.[16] Among the early Mongols there also seem to have been taboos associated with particular animals. Some could not be hunted at certain times of the year, while others, captured in the great battue hunts, were intentionally set free. Such custom had also the practical value of preserving wild animal stocks. The modern Kazakh word for a natural reserve, *qoryq*, originally designated a sacred area, often where some poten-

16 R. Berdibayev, personal communication, summer, 1991.

tate was buried, where animals could not be hunted out of respect for the soul of the diseased.[17]

Mongols and others, including the Chinese, believed that certain animals possessed special powers. As a consequence, once they had established their empires, they made a conspicuous display of eating exotic animals. By so doing they believed that they absorbed the power of the animal being eaten and thus increased their own.

Cultivated grain is uncommon almost everywhere on the steppe. It is rarely grown there, although some modern groups, including the Mongols, have tried to develop farming in part to provide for what is now a large urban population. During the era of the Mongolian empire, the conquerors sought to introduce a more regular cultivation by using captive farmers specially settled in Mongolia for that purpose, but because the same environmental constraints affecting growing grain in the steppe also affected such farming, these efforts were soon discontinued. Migrant farmers, usually Chinese, have also grown grain in areas adjacent to the Mongolian steppe and sometimes, when conditions were favorable and taking great environmental risks, actually in the steppe itself. Nonetheless, some traditional steppe groups do plant crops in the spring on their winter pastures, then leave them to go on their trek, and gather the harvest when they return in the autumn. Millet is specifically mentioned as being grown this way among the early Mongols. The anthropological theorist Alfred L. Kroeber characterized the Mongols as a "half-culture" since they were supposedly dependent upon sedentary grain to survive, but this was never actually the case.[18] The traditional diet, in all its aspects, provided a more than adequate basis for maintaining life. When steppe peoples consume grain, they generally do so by choice, not by necessity, except in those areas such as Inner Mongolia where a dominant majority forces its foods and food practices on the min-

---

[17] The Mongols also have a tradition of respect for the animals they herd and an unwillingness to overuse what nature provides in general terms. Mongol values in these areas are in strict contrast to Christian approach, the basis of most externally imposed development, which places man in control of nature with no questions asked in the event of overuse or waste.

[18] For a discussion of Kroeber and his views see Harris, 1984: 319ff and passim.

ority or restricts traditional sources of food so the steppe groups involved have no choice but to eat non-steppe foods.

The system described above has continued for the Mongols more or less down to the present day except that modern Mongolia has acquired a large, urban, and sedentary sector, along with manufacturing, mining and mineral extraction and other industries. Today, the traditional pastoral sector is smaller than it was in the nineteenth century and earlier, but it remains the heart of Mongolian national life and livelihood. This is true even if Mongolia's agricultural sector contributes less, on paper, to Mongolia's current GDP than in former times. Since 1900, Mongolian pastoralism has undergone many changes, without any of them having so far fundamentally altered its nature. During the 1920s and early 1930s, forced collectivization (Murphy, 1966: 92-130), carried to extremes, did threaten the very Mongolian way of life and resulted in enormous death and destruction, including of livestock, whose numbers took many years to recover. Nonetheless, despite the excesses of the era of forced collectivization, the traditional herdsman was not much disturbed during Mongolia's main Soviet period beginning in the late 1930s. There had been, at first, much opposition to outside control, even a major revolt in response to leftist excesses, but by the 1940s conditions had quieted. Russia, needing Mongolian food and other resources during the second world war, deemphasized the idealistic collectivization of traditional Mongolia (Murphy, 1966: 131-146). As a result, the cooperatives that finally emerged, the *negdel*, were often clan controlled and differed little from earlier pastoral systems (Saunders, 1996: 45-46). By 1959, 70% of the pastoral land was in the hands of such cooperatives (Saunders, *loc.cit.*). Other Mongolian land was controlled by state farms (Saunders, 1996: 105-106), in which members were employees, including a carefully supported grain production system that worked relatively well since it was fostered by the government and by the Soviet Union.

The final system that emerged in the People's Republic was thus very much a compromise with tradition. Communist institutions closely meshed with older kinship-based systems for regulating and coordinating pastoralism.[19] In the end, the Communists

[19] On how this worked out in general see Humphrey and Sneath, 1999: 68ff.

did not seriously threaten the traditional ways of doing things. Only specific institutions such as educational, health, and veterinary services were new and were supported by the central government. These services were provided at the *somon*[20] centers. The Commu nists were particularly successful in raising the living standards of the herdsmen, including literacy which is very high in Mongolia. In fact, it is unusually high for a developing country and could serve as a basis for further development of a new, industrial and urbanized Mongolia (see Fernandez-Gimenez, 1999; Sneath, 1999; 2002).

While the Communists, except during the era of Leftist deviation (1929-1932), never seriously threatened the Mongolian way of life, and helped provide a basis for a new way of life to exist in parallel with the traditional systems, rampant capitalism now does. In 1991 the Soviet Union collapsed and Mongolia gradually became a democracy. Gone were Soviet-era subsidies, leaving Mongolia scrambling since.[21] Also vanished was a system that protected collective as opposed to individual ownership of resources. For the last "2200 years of statehood in Mongolia, land has never been privately owed, but belonged to …highest body of legislature" (Tumenbayar). Now even this may change and land privatization, even pastoral land, has become a real issue.

In 1990, the Mongolian People's Revolutionary Party finally lost its monopoly on power after decades of one-party rule, although it still remained the single largest party in the Mongolian parliament or *Khural* and thus continued in power. An era of radical experimentation with capitalism and the market place began, fostered by the international organizations that moved in to replace the Soviet Union as Mongolia's guarantors. Serious dislocations resulted, the effects of which are still being felt today (Rossabi, 2005). The Communists finally lost power in 1996, but regained it in 2000 in a resounding success, only to lose it again in 2004. A coalition now governs, but one Communist president has now been replaced by another. Unfortunately, the Communists of today are not the Communists of pre-1991 and are also devoted to

---

[20] Mongolia is divided into *aimag*, or provinces, *somon*, equivalent to counties, and *bag*, the smallest units in the system. Most local services have been grouped at the *somon* centers.

[21] The best account of this era is now Rossabi, 2005: 1-79.

economic reform. Their position has been complicated by Mongolia's depressed state as a debtor, and thus they must follow the dictates of the World Bank, the International Monetary Fund, and other creditors and investors, and accept restraints imposed after Mongolia's first wild experiments with capitalism.

One result has been a general drive for privatization, which has proven to be the greatest threat ever to Mongolian traditional pastoralism because it is based upon individualistic assumptions that cannot be applied to a necessarily collectivist pastoralism. Although only livestock and equipment once belonging to the old cooperatives (*negdel*) have so far been privatized, there is pressure to privatize pastures too (Pocha, 2005). Unfortunately, individually held pastures, whatever the theory of land ownership behind them, and restricted movement of herds spell disaster, all the more so because Mongolia has serious environmental problems.[22] They are an issue in and of themselves, but the overuse of pastures that has resulted from privatization of livestock and a too rapid build-up of livestock numbers by individuals anxious to maximize their profits, regardless of the condition the pastures are in, has made them all the worse.

Privatization laws were enacted in 1992, so as to accord with the liberal economic reforms then being carried out by Mongolia's

---

[22] But not all of Mongolia's environmental problems are due to herding. Mining has, for example, devastated much Mongolian land and gold mining is a serious competitor with herding for scarce water resources. See the discussion in Rossabi, 2005: 175ff. See also Badarch, Batsukh and Batmunkh, 2003; Pocha, 2004. In 2000, Mongolia consumed some 443 million m^3 of water, equal to 1.5 percent of reserves, but water consumption, thanks to gold mining in particular, may now be up considerably. Mongolia's biggest water problem is in the Gobi, a naturally dry region where 60 percent of Mongolian wells are located, to serve around 200,000 herding households. These are too few wells serving too many (*EDN*, 24 March, 2003). Recently, as an indication of the scope of the problem, the Tuul River, from which most of Ulaanbaatar's drinking water comes, has begun to dry up. Falling water levels are primarily due to industrial use and there is increased water pollution due to the same origin as well (*EDN*, 15 May, 2002). In 2002, 42.5 percent of Mongolia's territory was threatened by desertification with moving sands having seized 1.44 million hectares of once productive land over the last thirty years, including much formerly useful pasture land, 70 percent of which have now been affected by sand intrusion (*EDN,* 20 December, 2002). This has lead to increased disputes over those pastures that have still not been degraded (*EDN*, 25 December, 2002).

democratic governments (*Jane's Sentinel*, 2004). These reforms were then seen as necessary to speed economic development and enhance a sustainable investment in land. They also met demands by the World Trade Organization and the World Bank as preconditions for those organizations to support Mongolia (*Jane's Sentinel*, 2004). Included as part of this reform effort were two other important reform laws, a revised Mongolian Constitution, and a new general Land Law.[23]

The new Mongolian Constitution was the first document in Mongolian history to enforce land entitlement institutions. The land is now essentially the property of the state, unless given to a citizen on the basis of private ownership. Even then, the state retains the power to confiscate land from landowners, who are responsible for the maintenance of land, and to order exchanges of land with compensation in order to meet certain state needs. The state may also confiscate land in order to ensure public health, the prevention of environmental degradation, and for reasons of national security. The new Constitution was followed by the 1994 Land Law. Mongolia's land is currently zoned by the Land Law, which has designated 76% for agriculture and grazing. The Law has allowed, under the Mongolian Constitution, state owned land to be leased to Mongolian citizens, businesses, and organizations for up to sixty years (Tumenbayar).

Privatization endorsing individual, not state, ownership of the means of production has been considered critical for Mongolia's capitalist development, and developmental aid has generally been formulated on a basis that is antagonistic to any collective ownership. Here the dominant influence has been Garret Hardin's famous "tragedy of the commons" idea:

> The tragedy of the commons develops in this way. Picture a pasture open to all. It is to be expected that each herdsman will try to keep as many cattle as possible on the commons... As a rational being, each herdsman seeks to maximize his gain...The rational herdsman concludes

---

[23] On Mongolian land reform see also Hanstad and Duncan, 2001. Most of the relevant documents have now been published by the Mongols in English translations.

> that the only sensible course for him to pursue is to add another animal to his herd. And another; and another... But this is the conclusion reached by each and every rational herdsman sharing a commons. Therein is the tragedy. Each man is locked into a system which compels him to increase his herd without limit — in a world that is limited. Ruin is the destination towards which all men rush, each pursuing his own interest in a society that believes in the freedom of the commons. Freedom in a commons brings ruin to all" (Stavins, 2000: 13)[24]

Though first discussed in 1968, the concept of the "tragedy of the commons" is still relevant when discussing the overgrazing problem in Mongolia. The maximization structure offered by capitalism, for example, with each herdsman striving to raise more and more animals, has destroyed a key area of Mongolia's traditional social capital, the cooperative institutions of Mongolia's pastoral way of life which has served as the traditional source of food for Mongolia. The ending of the old system has led, in essence, to impeded rights of entitlement to the food provided by livestock. In the past, if a herdsman wanted to keep many more livestock on common pastures, he would have had to negotiate with other users of the same pastures, usually meaning the rest of his clan. By contrast, in the capitalist system of Mongolia, the control over access is lost, for "[The] 1994 [Law] makes it impossible to prevent free-riding or to exclude outsiders from grazing" (Griffin, 2003c: 68). The huge number of deaths among livestock in recent years has been one result as the carrying capacities of many pastures have been exceeded.

The problem, as Fratkin and other critics of Hardin's idea point out is that commons are not truly commons. Ideally, in economic terms, commons are a common good with minimal costs accruing from their use, since these are spread finely over the maximum number of users. In fact, most of the world's commons, particularly pastoral lands used traditionally, are not even remotely an open, common good. There are significant marginal costs associ-

---

[24] In fairness to Hardin, he later modified and moderated his ideas and recognized the fact that the problem lay in unregulated commons. Unfortunately, it was Hardin's original idea that has had the greatest and most enduring influence.

ated with their use due to traditional controls and sanctions imposed on their users and over-users. In fact, if these controls and sanctions did not exist, the societies having the commons would mostly likely have themselves ceased to exist long ago. Overuse of common land would have destroyed the given environments that have formed the very basis for commons' use. In fact the only true commons in an economic sense are probably those created by the imposition of Hardin's ideas, where the traditional controls and sanctions have been done away with in the name of a misplaced development (see the discussion in Fratkin, 1997) and the rule of law needed to control the new use of formerly common lands has not yet emerged. This is precisely the problem in Mongolia.

Ever since the first emergence of the Mongols as a people with a history, there have been various mechanisms in place for controlling the use of pastures.[25] At the one level, the mechanisms have been political, for example, the assignment of pastures by higher authorities, including rulers and princes and, in later times, monasteries, and the control that all higher authorities have exercised over actual pastoral practices including movement (Bold, 2001; Fernandez-Gimenez, 1999). At the other, as Roux points out, religious beliefs, principally those involved with the worship of the spirits of the lands and waters, with sacred mountains and animals, have restrained pasture use and the use of other environmental resources. How this worked out in practice is seen in the recent example of the *negdel*. Although older religious ideas became somewhat submerged while not completely vanishing under the influence of Communist ideology, the *negdel* was until the end an effective means of regulating pastoralism within its jurisdiction and keeping pasture use under strict control. It worked in close accordance with the dictates of Mongolian society. The *negdel* was also an effective marketing mechanism, channeling the products of pastoralism to the center, where they could be further distributed. As already indicated, it also functioned as the basic Mongolian unit for social services, including, education, medical and other treatment, and even modern veterinary support (Fernandez-Gimé-

---

[25] On the general topic of the sustainability of pastoralism under Mongolian conditions see Sheehy, 1999. On pastoralism and livestock breeding see also Telenged, 1996.

nez, 1999; see also Bruun, 1999). Although a Communist institution, and associated with a modern world of medicine and education, in their work the *negdel* were not all that different from the religious units that controlled much of Mongolian society before 1911 or, for that matter, formerly existing princely domains. But now Mongolia has a true commons in every sense of the word, and such regulatory institutions no longer exist in the name of privatization, and the sanctions coming from below and from above are no longer sufficiently strong to prevent "tragedy." The result has been a paradox: the attempt to avoid the "tragedy of the commons" has been its very cause.

The important thing is that the old Communist structures are gone and the new land laws form the basis of property rights for a capitalistic society. They may, in the end, improve the Mongolian way of life under a capitalistic society. Nonetheless, it is still important to understand that the privatization provisions of the new land laws do not recognize the traditional land use of the herders or the traditional principle of collective or group ownership, since clans are not technically corporations, i.e. collective units whose rights are protected in Mongolian law (Tumenbayar). Traditional herders being the main force behind the land, there is an apparent disconnect between economic structure encompassing anti-herding practices and a system of social capital which has dealt with geographic restraints of Mongolia.

Since privatization was introduced, Mongolia's main source of agriculture is still livestock. Some 88% of Mongolian agriculture is related to pastoralism (Griffin, 1997). Unfortunately, as much as 95% of Mongolia's land is classified by some as highly vulnerable to desertification, and the size of Mongolia's deserts grows each year, which is a visible phenomenon (Tumenbayar), although there are varied explanations of precisely what is taking place and even of the actual size of the phenomenon. Although the media and scholars have generally explained privatization in terms of overgrazing by the herder (Griffin, 1997; 2003c: 33; Leicester; Tumenbayar), this reason merely scratches the surface. As Griffin has put it: "The claim of widespread overgrazing is…exaggerated." In fact, while grazing has increased for some land, it has decreased for other (Griffin, 2003c: 70), in part due to a decline in distances migrated as part of a normal pastoral regimen (Fernandez-Giménez,

1999; Sneath, 2002). This is due to the decreased support available for migration itself and to inexperienced herdsmen, including many forced out of Mongolia's swollen cities back to the land, trying their hands at livestock raising, for good or ill (Sneath, 1999; 2002). Thus the true issue is the concentration of intensified land use which has been caused by the structural issues emerging from privatization.

The concentration of pastoralism on limited lands is Mongolia's post-Soviet problem. It has been caused primarily by rural decline due to the mass migration of herdsmen to the northern areas of the country, where there are more jobs outside agriculture. Life is more comfortable there in the larger established settlements with such amenities as heating systems and thick-walled apartments. Nonetheless, although many herdsmen are attracted to the north for reasons of comfort and opportunity, leading to rural dislocation and even labor shortages, the main issues with the changes taking place all involve the transformation into a free market system.

Extracting minerals for trade has been the main focus of Mongolian governments since liberalization,[26] and has pushed for the creation of numerous settlements, actually small rural shanty towns, to appear along the northern border with Russia in order to transport the minerals to the railways needed for shipping. In addition, by placing most of its social resources within these settlements, the government has unintentionally encouraged the migration of herdsmen to the North. During the Soviet era, resources were concentrated in local settlements, primarily *somon* centers, to encourage some sedentarization that would enhance the control over the nomads. Since 1991 and the final collapse of the Soviet Union, these settlements, because they have relatively more resources than other sites, combined with the new ability of herdsmen migrate freely, are being taxed to serve the local population in ways never intended while at the same time they are themselves in decline and even in the process of disappearance. The migration north has only been intensified since the new government has allowed wells to dry up in the Gobi, and veterinary services and int-

---

[26] See, however, the recent summary provided in Badarch, Batsukh and Batmunkh, 2003. Minerals have not always provided the greatest amount of short-term foreign exchange, even if emphasized in terms of capital investment.

ermediary livestock transport of the past have all but disappeared outside the larger settlements (Griffin, 2003b: 65-66).

To make matter worse, the Law on Land Fees, passed in 1997, has placed an additional burden on settlement land. It allows the exemption from grazing fees and offers a tax exemption of fifty *tugrik*, now worth a few cents, for every animal produced, thereby encouraging herders to raise more animals than the land can maintain. Whereas in 1990, there were only 75,000 herdsman families, that figure increased to 187,000 in 2000. This is a more than a 100% increase of users of a land that has already been stressed by past increases in numbers of herders. However, as Tumenbayar observes, "new entrants to the herding communities are constrained in gaining access to pastures, as they tend to have much less developed kinship and other social networks and have greater tendency to remain sedentary". This has meant more pastures closer to the settlements with a resulting increase in pasture damage and desertification. This dire scenario was created by the improper use of pastures that is slowly destroying the most important means of access to food in Mongolia.

While the rural lands are facing their own problems, cities have also begun to reflect the negative effects of the Land Law. Ulaanbaatar, the capital, is the only true modern city in contemporary Mongolia and may soon or already have a population exceeding one million. In and around the city the importance of livestock and the degradation of land is evident. According to Tumenbayar, in 1990 Ulaanbaatar contained only 76,000 private livestock, but this figure increased to 301,000 in 1998.[27] The increase of land use involved has led to lands next to the city, as is the case with the settlements, becoming overgrazed. To make matters worse, the dust blown up from the degraded pastures has been added to the soot and smoke emanating from cooking stoves that are using

[27] A somewhat lower figure of 233,000 is given for the end of 2002 but this is likely an underestimate (*EDN*, 8 January, 2003; 10 April, 2003). This trend may accelerate in the future since it is now official policy to promote an intensified animal husbandry close to the large population centers, in part because of the problem of marketing distantly produced food and other agricultural products. Among those enunciating this policy was former Prime Minister N. Enkhbayar, See *EDN*, 11 March, 2002; 19 May, 2003; BBC (Asian-Pacific, 24 October, 2003).

dung, wood and coal, making Ulaanbaatar one of the most polluted cities in the world (*Jane's Sentinel*, 2004).

While desertification and pasture degradation have endangered the future development of food production, the movement of people to herding or city jobs has also diverted resources from grain farming, thereby deepening food insecurity (Tumenbayar; Sneath, 2002). In the 1950s, the government began to form large to midsized grain farms which increased domestic grain production and thereby lessened the need for imported grain. Now, in accordance with the Land Law, the land has been fragmented into small units whose owners do not have the capital to properly maintain their fields which, according to Tumenbayar, have greatly deteriorated. As a result, Mongolia's grain production fell from 718,000 tons in 1990 to 195,000 tons in 1998 (Sneath, 2002: 196) all the way down to 106,900 tons in 2002 (*Jane's Sentinel*, 2004), before slightly improving to 165,000 tons in 2003 (*Statistikiyn Emkhtgel*, 2003)[28] The result of this calamitous downturn has been that Mongolia now has to import grain, something it did not do regularly under Soviet sponsorship (*Jane's Sentinel*, 2004; Griffin, 1997). Mongolia suffers as a result, since funds are lacking to import all the grain needed. Some 139,300 tons of wheat were imported in 2002, and although this figure fell to only 61,500 tons in 2003 (*Statistikiin Emkhtgel*, 2003), not all of the decline can be accounted for by increased Mongolian production. In any case, importation of flour has remained particularly high, 75,200 tons in 2003, compared to 96,900 tons in 2002 (*Statistikiin Emkhtgel*, 2003).[29] Demand

[28] In addition, 65,446 tons of potatoes and 24,596 tons of vegetables were harvested in 2002, figures well below Mongolia's minimal needs. Not only were harvests smaller in that year, but 2 million head of livestock were also lost (*EDN*, 15 January, 2003). In 2003, in addition to the nearly 165,000 tons of wheat, 78,000 tons of potatoes and 58,100 tons of vegetables and about 3,000 tons of other grain crops were harvested. Of the wheat, 29,400 tons was to be reserved for 2004 seed. This is a high figure. The Mongolian harvest for 2003 was said to meet approximately 30 percent of its flour needs, 52 percent of its potato needs, and 31 percent of its vegetable needs (*EDN*, 27 August, 2003; 19 November, 2003).

[29] Other food imports by Mongolian in 2003, that is, beside wheat and flour, included 100 tons of vegetable oil, 3,000 tons of margarine, and 19,000 tons of sugar, 5,100 tons of candy, 5,200 tons of "flavored flour products," 100 tons of canned fruits and nuts, 14,800 tons of rice, 1,900 tons of tea, 23,300 tons of

for both grain and flour will continue to grow rapidly since a growing urban population generally lacks the production wherewithal to supplement limited grain foods with those from an active pastoralism. That is to say, Mongolia's position in these areas will only grow worse with each passing year.

Although Mongolia continues to export food, like beef to the former Soviet Union (*Jane's Sentinel*, 2004), as a result of various pastoral dislocations described in the preceding paragraphs, the country has nonetheless gained recognition in the media as being a center of hunger. Headlines such as "Mongolia Herdsmen Face Starvation" (BBC News, 14 March, 2000), "Alarm over Food Crisis" (BBC News, 28 June, 2000), "Mongolia's People, Tradition Threatened by Disastrous Winter" (Leicester) are common in articles relating to hunger in Mongolia, that often describe its vast emptiness and the dangers encountered by Mongolia's sparse inhabitants. To be sure, these headlines are connected with the severe *dzud* conditions of the early part of this decade as animals were unable to feed due to blizzard conditions or severe icing but the main reason why millions of animals died in single years was a too rapid increase of herds under conditions of privatization of ownership that encouraged the raising of too many animals beyond the capacities of the pastures and the pastoral infrastructure, which continues to be in decline, to support them.

Some of the metaphor used in such press reports might lead the reader into believing that the source of hunger is Malthusian: Mongolia simply has too few resources to maintain its current population, thus the hunger, but this interpretation gives an entirely false impression. The true issue is the structural changes that have taken place in Mongolia since the end of Mongolia's Soviet period in 1991, when subsidies and protectionism began to disappear and the pastoral infrastructure and marketing mechanism began to crash (*Jane's Sentinel*, 2004; Sneath, 1999; 2002; Fernandez-Giménez, 1999).

---

fresh fruit, 5 million liters of soft drinks, and 17.2 million liters of alcoholic beverages, of soft drinks, commodities not usually produced in Mongolia, but also 55,100 tons of butter, a very high figure, and up substantially over the previous year, 40,200 additional tons of potatoes, 7,100 tons of onions and garlic, which can be produced locally, and 6,200 tons of millet, which also can be produced locally.

Mongolia has since the beginning of recorded history been a country dedicated to pastoralism, and has not experienced real hunger as a nation until the last decade. Against Malthusian theory, Mongolia's population has begun to increase far more slowly than in the recent past, and growth has been quite moderate during the present occurrence of hunger. In fact, Mongolia's period of rapid population growth, marking a recovery from a low point in the twentieth century, was under the Communists and during that period living standards actually improved. There was no hunger. Since then the rate of population increase has dropped from 2.9% in 1980 to 1.4% in 2000 (Griffin, 2003a: 6). It has, since leveled off (*Jane's Sentinel*, 2004) at about that plateau, barely a replacement rate when the aging of the Mongolian population is taken into account and likely future growth rates if present trends continue.[30] The statistics thus show a 51.7% decrease in the true population growth rate (Griffin, 2003a: 5). Therefore, Malthusian theory simply does not explain Mongolia's problems since population pressure is now minimal in a country that was sparsely populated to begin with.

To be sure, one could strengthen the Malthusian argument by pointing to environmental problems, principally the continued expansion of Mongolia's deserts and ground contamination caused by gold and other mining activities, that have reduced the total amount of Mongolian pasture. Moreover, the climate may be worsening, with the frequent *dzud* having been particularly severe in recent years (BBC News, 14 March, 2000; *Jane's Sentinel*, 2004). While each of these environmental problems has contributed to hunger in Mongolia, the main reason why Mongolia has faced real hunger in the last decade or so, is its turn to a free-market economy, a change that has had a strong adverse impact not only upon Mongolian pastoralism, but even on its limited grain agriculture.

---

[30] The reasons for the decline in the population growth rate are many. Economic conditions today are certainly factors but the fact that Mongolia is becoming increasingly urban and urban populations are more likely to restrain births is clearly a factor too. The death rate will rise as the population ages further decreasing the growth rate if fertility remains the same.

THE FORGOTTEN WAY OF LIFE

Mongolia's shift to a free market has not only dislocated Mongolian society in fundamental ways, physically shifting its population and resources around and dislocating links, but it is also slowly undermining Mongolia's traditional modes of production. These are urgently needed if Mongolia is to produce enough food under sharply limiting environmental conditions.

Over the centuries Mongols have developed an intricate web, a key part of their traditional social capital, for food access. Like other Eurasian pastoralists, most Mongols have remained almost totally dependent on their livestock. Their traditional foods have been largely and nearly exclusively what Mongol pastoralists can gain and consume from animals, usually without seriously depleting their herds. In practical terms, this has meant a variety of fermented dairy products some of which, when dried, last virtually forever, thus allowing dairy products to be stored indefinitely.[31] Other foods, including rare meat, grains and grain foods consumed by preference to break the monotony of a primarily dairy food diet, play only a minor role.[32] The Mongolian diet is not a rich nor certainly a varied one but it is more than adequate, and it is ideally suited to local conditions and given environmental resources. In thousands of years, no one has much improved on it.

Aligned with this diet, and in part to sustain its production, Mongolia has pursued its highly complex pastoral support system, directly involving everyone in the community. This system is now breaking down. In the past, the system nearly always involved movement in regular cycles, often over quite large distances, as re-

---

[31] Fresh milk production was 3.1 million liters during the first eight months of 2003, but Mongols rarely consume dairy products fresh. See *EDN*, 7 November, 2003.

[32] The Mongols do now fish on a large scale, licenses being issued for a catch of 21,000 tons in 2003. Much of this appears to be exported (*EDN*, 12 May, 2003). Gathering of plant foods also continues, including buckthorn fruits, which are also cultivated, and probably pine nuts and other nuts, although most of those collected may be exported (*EDN*, 19 August, 2003; 4 December, 2003). Also a source of supplemental food for the Mongols is hunting. Some 58,593 marmots were taken in 2003, along with far smaller numbers of larger animals, although most of these go to foreign hunters who pay for the privilege of hunting in Mongolia (*EDN*, 3 December, 2003).

quired by sustainability, usually by small groups of herdsmen moving and camping along with their livestock. In the Soviet period, herding families were grouped into larger units during the colder months of the year, when they most often camped next to towns which provided education to their young and social services to everyone. This was part of the *negdel* system (see Fernandez-Giménez, 1999).

Thus during the winter and spring herding families were usually established at a permanent camping site, situated at a low altitude in order to find more protected shelter for livestock birth in the early spring. The true nomadic life, by contrast, was expressed during summer and autumn when the herdsmen created small nomadic camps, usually at higher altitudes, called *hot ail.* They included two to eight families on average. Depending on the specific natural circumstances of their local environments -- mountain pasture (*hangai)*, semi-desert (gobi), desert (*els)*, dry plains, river valleys, etc. -- the *hot ail* could separate for part of the summer-autumn herding season. The *ail* formed the foundation for societal communal land use, for within this family unit the distribution of resources, most significantly pasture land and water wells, took place (Buell, Anderson, and Perry, 2000: 30-34; Fernandez-Giménez, 1999). This remains the case even today, although the structure of families has often changed, in part due to the return of unemployed relatives from the city, and movement is usually now only over short distances.

Under Mongolian conditions, resources are usually too limited for groups to compete with one another, although this is another area of traditional Mongolian life that is now changing rapidly. In the past, usage was carefully coordinated over a larger region leading *hot ail* to form larger social networks called *neg goliinhon* or *neg nutgiinhan.* They were co-users of a pastoral environment and established the right to land use for all participating herdsmen (Tumenbayar). Generally speaking, these larger social networks were clan-based (Buell, Anderson and Perry, 2000: 30-34). There were no exclusive, private rights of individual herdsmen over land use.[33] The land remained a communal property and the individual herdsman had to be connected to a group, for example through kinship,

[33] This facet of pastoral society is discussed in particular detail in Tolybekov.

in order to gain access to the land and its pastoral resources. Since higher-level groups coordinated pasture land use, a herdsman was prohibited from grazing without the approval of the *neg goliinhon* or *neg nutgiinhan*. If conflicts over land issues did occur, oral agreements were made to resolve the issue, intermediated, if necessary, by clan or group elders or, in more recent times, by local officials at the *somon* or even *aimag* level (Fernandez-Giménez, 1999; Bold, 2001). The *negdel* usually coincided with the *somon*, although having its own governing body.

This is the part of pastoralism in Mongolia that has now more or less collapsed, with devastating results. Herding units still exist, but they are now little coordinated beyond a basic level with severe negative consequences for the environment and herding in general. By contrast with today, traditional Mongolian society was sensitive to the limitations of the land, and the ways in which traditional herdsmen have used it have involved a complex system of sustainable exploitation by careful regulation of the usage of space in time. In addition, the Mongols have obviously developed a diet that works for them and a pastoral system to support it. This system, by tradition, entitled everyone within a group or kinship unit to access to pasture in some form or the other, even when primarily herding someone else's animals, and to pastoralism's main product, food, which by Mongolian tradition had to be shared.[34]

In short, traditional Mongolian society offered a highly developed system of social capital, now being eroded. It allowed for subsistence in harsh terrain through providing the essentials of life: housing (covered by felt made from sheep's wool), clothing (felt and skins), water (cooperatively controlled wells and other sources, food and, most important, the right not to go hungry. This is in addition to social capital in the form of mutual assistance provided in herding and other forms of social networking promoting survival and effective pastoralism.

---

[34]Contributing to the sharing of food in Mongolian society is its nature. A Mongolian sheep, usually small, when slaughtered provides just about enough meat to feed a family. Traditionally, any left over meat is given to neighbors ensuring distribution across families (Buell, Anderson, and Perry, 2000: 30-34). It will not keep otherwise. The same has been true for many seasonal foods such as kumiss, available for only a relatively short time and thus to be shared.

MARKETING ISSUES

Most of this is now gone. Much of the higher organization of Mongolian society has now vanished and even the ways in which pastoralism is done have changed (Sneath, 1999; 2002; Fernandez-Giménez, 1999). Although land remains, in theory, common, livestock are not in any way, as was once the practice. All have been divided up after the demise of the *negdel*, meaning that present herds are individually owned and pastured.

There are two main problems with this. One is that movements are now over a shorter distance, in part because the support network that the *negdel* once provided in assisting movements no longer exists. Even when individuals have taken over vehicles once belonging to the *negdel* they often cannot maintain them, since gasoline and diesel fuel have become far more expensive, when available at all, not to mention spare parts. There is also the problem, and here lies the "tragedy," that individuals, in order to maximize profits, try to keep more animals even if their resources will not support them. There are also far more herdsmen now, as the unemployed return from local centers and cities, anxious to compete for their own right to exist (Sneath, 1999; 2002; Fernandez-Giménez, 1999).

These facts and the reduced movements mean that the negative impact of the current pastoralism on the environment is now far greater than before. Some pastures are being used to exhaustion, others barely. Secondly, the *negdel* was also the means by which local products were channeled, sometimes through forced requisitions, a form of taxation, from the pastoral sector to the center, particularly Mongolia's towns and cities. Now the forces of the market place apply but the market does not really work.[35] Most products produced locally remain local, resulting in a shortage of

---

[35] This is not only true for food marketing. Mongolia's wool and skin processing industries were only operating at a 5-40 percent capacity at the beginning of 2003 due of a shortage of basic raw materials and uncontrolled exports, meaning the raw materials were being trucked over the border in a raw state to meet *ad hoc* demands by-passing local processors (*EDN*, 23 January 2003). Also an indication of marketing dislocation to some degree, although the need for foreign exchange is important too, is Mongolia's continuing exportation of meat, about 20,000 tons annual, nearly all of it to Russia (*EDN*, 24 January 2003).

food products at the national level. Instead of a plethora of dairy products, which should have been the logical result of more herdsmen and more animals, there is now a shortage and the present system, in part due to large-scale losses of livestock on account of concentrated overuse of limited pastures, is far less efficient than the old. Environmental pressures have thus increased but there is no real gain from them, while the prices for those foods reaching the national market have gone up considerably, as has everything else.

Thus Mongolia's enforced worship of the market place has resulted to a great degree in a collapse of the market locally. In most respects, when we also take into consideration the high prices that people in the pastoral sector must pay for just about anything they do not produce and consume, government policy has resulted in deep economic isolation. A dangerous cycle has developed in Mongolia: the country must now import more food, but the cost of this food is competing with the cost of industrial goods needed to develop Mongolia so that it can become less dependent upon its own pastoralism.[36] That is to say, inept policy threatens the very thing that Mongolia needs to survive in the future as well as in the present (Sneath, 1999; 2002; Fernandex-Giménez, 1999; see also Rossabi, 2005).

---

[36] Aware of this, Mongolia briefly imposed a 15 percent import tariff on imported potatoes, cabbages, beets, carrots and flour between 1 August, 2003 and 1 April, 2004, but such responses only make the problem worse since shortages remain and prices will rise to match greater import costs (*EDN*, 28 July, 2003). To supplement limited locally produced wheat, the United States supplied 24,500 tons in 2003 as a grant (*EDN*, 31 July, 2003). Japan was to supply another 20,000 tons in 2003 and a purchase of 40,000 tons from Russia was later under consideration. Formerly, wheat was purchased from Kazakhstan but this has proven far too expensive for the Mongols (*EDN*, 5 March, 2001; 27 August, 2003). The Mongols currently consume about 240,000 tons of flour a year, about 30 percent of which was to come from domestic production of wheat in 2003 (*EDN*, 7 October, 2003). Apparently 300,000 tons of high quality wheat need to be raised to produce this much flour (*EDN*, 30 October, 2003). Nonetheless, even if Mongolia produces wheat at this level again, it may still import cheaper Chinese and Russian flour, undermining local production (*EDN*, 28 November, 2003). The deficit of wheat and flour in Mongolia were estimated at 167,500 tons and 122,400 tons respectively at the end of 2003 (*EDN*, 31 December, 2003).

JUDGMENT DAY

We have argued that the social dislocation and resulting hunger characterizing much of Mongolia today is the result of structural changes and the inability for the Mongols to adapt themselves to a newly formed capitalistic society that has emerged since 1990. Mongolia, in short, simply does not have the right kind of social capital to respond to new conditions. In fact, when traditional social capital is applied in the new environment it is often construed as corruption and is regarded entirely negatively, as if it were something out of place. That is to say, the very traits and interactions that make the Mongols so potentially successful in a pastoral environment is counter-productive in an urban, industrialized environment.[37] A new system of appropriate social capital for the new economic and social environment has yet to emerge, and until it does traditional values will run largely counter to what is required for it to be a part of the modern world.

Hence, in Mongolia, a country known for group collaboration in the form of clan control over resources, particularly pastures (Buell, Anderson, Perry, 2000: 27-35), traditional communalism is not in sync with the need to develop in a capitalistic society, with individuals functioning through self-interest rather than through group decision. Yet it is group decision that has been the basis of Mongolia's past success in feeding its people with limited geographic resources and has prevented, through group censure, the "tragedy of the commons" arising through overuse of fragile pasture resources. In short, liberalization has undermined much social stability and curtailed access to food, a social necessity, by stressing individual over social needs. It leaves people ill fitted to function under new conditions because of a lack of social capital and to develop and sustain an economic system that is able to feed the hungry and sustain them socially.

In addition, hunger produced by scarcity is deepened by the poverty and inequality prevalent in all capitalistic societies. In the traditional pastoral system, inequality was low, but privatization of

---

[37] One example is the practice of living in yurts and trying to herd animals right in the city. This practice has meant not only a lower standard of living for the urban migrant but also a highly polluted urban environment. Cattle wandering free along the main streets does not work very well in a large city, alas.

the once communal livestock has created vast inequalities, with the herders having the most experience and political power receiving most of the livestock. In 1992, the top 5% of the largest herders held 200 animals, while the bottom 42%, comprised of female-headed households and young herders, had on average thirty-one animals (Griffin, 2003b: 18). Since then the situation has further deteriorated, not so much because the number of animals per household has fallen, but primarily because the cost of everything else has skyrocketed.[38] In a society that still bases most food access through livestock, the inequality inherent in capitalism has certainly destroyed the food security for the common Mongol. The ultimate question is whether or not it will also destroy Mongolian society as a whole.[39]

CONCLUSION: A RACE AGAINST TIME

What should Mongolia do? The answer is to pay heed to the past while planning for the future. Owen Lattimore many years ago pointed out that the most efficient use of Mongolia's territory is for pastoral nomadism, and that for ecological reasons grain agriculture will never take root on more than a limited or temporary basis (Lattimore, 1962). To feed themselves from their pastoralism, Mongols have had to develop a highly complex system of seasonal land use, which has proved to be the most productive possible land use, given the country's geographical conditions. The drive towards privatization, stressing individual rather than group ownership of land, is slowly destroying the traditional system of land use and with it food production, thereby creating substantial social dislocation and hunger in Mongolia. Mongolia is rich in mineral resources, and profits from these minerals could be used to supp-

[38] In 2002, while 87.5 percent of all families of herds owned 200 or so animals, the lowest standard for survival was then set at 390 head and those families having the average of 200 or so were considered potentially poor, although some were involved in other occupations as well as herding. Only 2.5 percent of all herding households were then considered well off and 47.8 percent were officially poor (*EDN*, 11 August, 2003). At the end of 2001, 639 families had 1000-1499 head, thirty-eight had 1500-2000, and thirty-one had more than 2000 (*EDN* , 29 January, 2002).

[39] See also examples and information in Rossabi, 2005: 132ff and passim.

lement Mongolia's existing food production, even if it declines further. The question, however, is whether these resources will be developed quickly enough, given Mongolia's infrastructure problems, to compensate for a decline in domestic food production. If they are not developed rapidly enough, hunger may turn into starvation in wide areas of Mongolia. This is the process that Mongolia's government has to deal with as it seeks to develop privatization further in response to the demands of the capitalistic world market. We are not advocating in this paper that Mongolia should abandon its path of modernization, but simply to moderate it. Nothing less than Mongolia's national survival is at stake in a world in which little Mongolia is being stared at intensely by two giants, Russia and China.

BIBLIOGRAPHY

Algar, Ayla. *Classical Turkish Cooking*. New York: HarperCollins Publishers, 1991.

Arsel, Semahat, Ersu Pekin, and Ayşe Sümer, eds. *Timeless Tastes: Turkish Culinary Culture*. 2nd ed. Istanbul: Divan Hotel, 1996. (Vehbi Koç Vakfı, publication No. 7)

Badarch, Dendeviin, Raymond A. Zilinskas, and Peter J. Balint, eds. *Mongolia Today: Science, Culture, Environment and Development*. London: RoutledgeCurzon, 2003.

_______, Naidanjiin Batsukh and Sereeteriin Batmunkh. "The Impacts of Industrialization in Mongolia." In Badarch, Zilinskas, and Balint, eds., 2003: 3-20.

Batbuyan, B. "Proposal for the Adoption of Ecologically Appropriate Regions for Herding in Inner Mongolia." In Humphrey and Sneath, eds., 1996, I: 198-208.

BBC News. "Mongolian Herdsmen Face Starvation." (World: Asian-Pacific, 14 March, 2000). In http://www.bbc.co.uk/.

_______. "Alarm Over Mongolia Food Crisis" (World: Asian-Pacific, 28 June, 2000). In http://www.bbc.co.uk/.

_______. "Mongolian Normadism 'To Die Out.'" (World: Asian-Pacific, 24 October, 2003). In http://www.bbc.co.uk/.

Bold, Bat-Ochir. *Mongolian Nomadic Society : A Reconstruction of the 'Medieval' History of Mongolia*. Richmond, Surrey: Curzon, 2001.

Brenner, Mark D. "Poverty in Mongolia." In Griffin, ed., 2003a: 29-55.

Bruun, Ole. "The Herding Household: Economy and Organization." In Kotkin and Elleman, eds., 1999: 65-89.

Buell, Paul D. " Steppe Foodways and History," *Asian Medicine: Tradition and Modernity*, 2.2, forthcoming

_______. "China's Grip on Mongolia," *Jane's Foreign Report*, 2851, 29 September, 2005, 6-7.

_______. "Popoli e Ciba della Steppa." In Massimo Montanari, and Françoise Sabban, eds.., *Atlante dell'Alimentazione e della Gastronomia.* 2 volumes. Torino: UTET, 2004, I, 242-257.

_______. "Mongolian Cuisine." In David Levinson, ed., *Encyclopedia of Asia.* Great Barrington, MA.: Berkshire Reference Works, 2002.

_______, and Eugene N. Anderson, Charles Perry. *A Soup for the Qan: Chinese Dietary Medicine of the Mongol Era as Seen in Hu Szu-hui's Yin-shan Cheng-yao,* introduction, translation, text, notes. Kegan Paul International (Sir Henry Wellcome Asian Series), London, 2000.

_______. "Mongolian Empire and Turkicization: The Evidence of Food and Foodways" In Reuven Amitai-Preiss ed., *The Mongol Empire and its Legacy* (Amsterdam: E.J. Brill, 1999), 200-223.

CIA World Factbook. In http://www.cia.gov/cia/publications/factbook/geos/mg.html. Accessed on May 25, 2005.

Damrinbazar, et. al. *Mongolyn ideen tovchoo*, 1987. Reprint: Ulaanbaatar: BNMAU Shinzhlekh ukhaany khevlel, 1991.

EDN (edn@magicnet.mn). Ulaanbaatar, Mongolia. Accessed during the years 2000 and 2003. Discontinued.

Erdenebaatar, B. "Socio-Economic Aspects of the Pastoral Movement Patterns of Mongolian Herders." In Humphrey and Sneath, eds., 1996, I, 58-110.

Erdenijab, E. 1996a. "An Economic Assessment of Pasture Degradation." In Humphrey and Sneath, eds., 1996, I: 189-197.

_______. 1996b. "On the Future of the Pastoral Economy: "Man, Society and Nature." In Humphrey and Sneath, eds., 1996, II: 102-115.

Fernandez-Giménez, Maria E. "Sustaining the Steppes: A Geographical History of Pastoral Land Use in Mongolia." *Geographical Review* 89 : 4 (July, 1999), 315-342.

Fratkin, Elliot. "Pastoralism: Governance and Development Issues." *Annual Review of Anthropology*, 26 (1997), 235-261.

Griffin, Keith, ed., 2003a. *Poverty Reduction in Mongolia*. Canberra: Asia Pacific Press (the Australian National University).

_______. 2003b. "The Macroeconomics of Poverty." In Griffin, ed., 2003a: 1-28.

_______. 2003c. "Urban-Rural Migration and Involution in the Livestock Sector." In Griffin, ed., 2003a, 56-71.

_______. FAO Crop and Food Supply Assessment Mission to Mongolia (1997). In http://216.239.57.104/search?q=cache: gswYHEDFFAJ: www.fao.org/docrep/004/w6668e/ w6668e00.htm+FAO+crop+and+food+supply +Assessment + Mission+to+Mongolia&hl=en&ie=UTF-8.

Hanstad, Tim and Jennifer Duncan. *Land Reform in Mongolia: Observations and Recommendations*. Seattle: Rural Development Institute (RDI Reports on Foreign Aid and Development, #109), 2001.

Harris, Marvin. *The Rise of Anthropological Theory*. New York: Columbia University, 1984

Humphrey, Caroline, and David Sneath, eds. *Culture and Environment in Inner Asia*. Two volumes. Cambridge: The White Horse Press, 1996.

_______ and David Sneath. *The End of Nomadism?: Society, State and the Environment in Inner Asia*. Durham: Duke University Press, 1999.

Ickowitz, Amy. "Poverty and the Environment." In Griffin, ed., *Poverty Reduction in Mongolia* 2003a: 95-112.

Indra, Rinchingiin. "Mongolian Dairy Products." In Badarch, Zilinskas and Balint, eds., 2003: 69-85.

Jauhiainen, Erkki. "Desertification and Pastoralism in Mongolia," in Sharma, R.C., ed., *Mongolia: Tryst with Change and Development*." Patiala: Vision and Venture, 1997, 239-252.

Jane's Sentinel, Security Assessment, China and Northeast Asia (subscription). In http://www.janes.com.

Kotkin, Stephen, and Bruce A. Elleman. *Mongolia in the Twentieth Century: Landlocked Cosmopolitan*. Armonk: M. E. Sharpe, 1999.

Lattimore, Owen. "The Geographical Factor in Mongol History." In O. Lattimore, *Studies in Frontier History, Collected Papers, 1929-1958*. London: Oxford University Press, 1962, 241-258.

Leicester, John. "Mongolia's People, Traditions Threatened by Disastrous Winter." *Friends of Mongolia "Zud" Digest*, No. 2, 17 March 2001. In http://www.friendsofmongolia.org.

Mandel, Ruth and Caroline Humphrey. *Markets and Moralities, Ethnographies of Postsocialism*. Oxford and New York: Berg, 2002.

McKinley, Terry. "The Governance Dimensions of Poverty Reduction." In Griffin, ed., 2003a: 113-131.

Mongolia, Mineral Resources and Petroleum Authority. *The Mining Journal*, 24 March, 2005, Focus, 27.

_______, National Statistical Office. *Monthly Bulletin of Statistics*, January, 2003.

_______, _______. *"Mongol Uls Zakh Zeeld," Statistikiin Emkhtgel, 1989-2002*. Ulaanbaatar, 2004.

_______, _______. *Mongol Ulsyn Statistikiyn Emkhtgel 2003*. Ulaanbaatar, 2004.

Murphy, George G. S. *Soviet Mongolia, A Study of the Oldest Political Satellite*. Berkeley and Los Angeles: University of California Press, 1966.

Namjim, Tumuriin. *The Economy of Mongolia: From Traditional Times to the Present*. Edited by William Rozycki. Bloomington: The Mongolia Society, Inc. (Occasional Papers Number 22), 2000.

Oyunbayar. "Meat, Milk and Mongolia: Misunderstood and Often Maligned, the Mongolian Diet Does Make Sense." *Ger Magazine* 2. In http://www.un-mongolia/mn/archives/ger-mag/issue2/foot.htm.

Pocha, Jehangir S. "In Mongolia 'Ninjas' Struggle to Make a Living, Thousands Give up Herding to Pan for Gold." *The Boston Globe*, 6 November, 2004. In http://www.boston.com/news/world/asia/articles/2004/11/06/in_mongolia_ninjas_struggle_to make_a-living (accessed on 6 December, 2004)

_______. "Mongolians Test Alien Idea: Privatizing the Land." *International Herald Tribune*, May 27, 2005, News, 2.

Qatran, Dosymbek. *Qazaqtyng Dasturli As-Tagham Madenieti (Tarikhi-Etnologiyalyq Zertteu)*, Almaty: Qazaqtyng Madeniet zhane Onertanu Ghylymi-Zertteu Instituty, 2002.

Rachewiltz, Igor de. *Index to the Secret History of the Mongols* (Uralic and Altaic Series 121). Bloomington: Indiana University Publications, 1972.

Riasanovsky, Valentin A. *Fundamental Principles of Mongol Law*. Bloomington: Indiana University, 1965. (Uralic and Altaic Series 43).

Rinchen, B. *Mongol ard ulsyn ugsaatny sudlal, khelniy shinzhleliyn atlas.* 2 vols. Ulaanbaatar, 1979.

Rossabi, Morris. *Modern Mongolia: From Khans to Commissars to Capitalists.* Berkeley, Los Angeles, London: University of California Press, 2005.

Roux, Jean-Paul. *Faune et Flore Sacrées dans les Sociétés Altaïques.* Paris: Librairie d'Amérique et d'Orient Adrien-Maisonneuve, 1966.

Saunders, Alan J. K. *Historical Dictionary of Mongolia.* Lanham and London: Scarecrow Press, 1996. (Asian Historical Dictionaries, 19).

Sen, Amartya. *Development as Freedom.* New York: Anchor Books, 1999.

Sheehy, Dennis P. "Sustainable Livestock Use of Pastoral Resources." In Kotkin and Elleman, eds., 1999: 42-64.

Sneath, David. "Mobility, Technology, and Decollectivization of Pastoralism in Mongolia." In Kotkin and Elleman, 1999: 223-236.

_______. "Mongolia in the 'Age of the Market': Pastoral Land-use and the Development Discourse." In Mandel and Humphrey, eds., 2002: 191-210.

Sobel, Joel. "Can We Trust Social Capital?" *Journal of Economic Literature* 40 :1 (March 2002), 139-154.

Stavins, Robert N., ed.. *Economics of the Environment: Selected Readings.* Fourth Edition. New York and London: W. W. Norton and Company, 2000.

Sitglitz, Joseph E. *Globalization and Its Discontents.* New York and London: W. W. Norton and Company, 2003.

Telenged, B. "Livestock Breeding in Mongolia Past and Present: The Advantages and Disadvantages of Traditional and Modern Animal Breeding Practices." In Humphrey and Sneath, eds., 1996, I: 161-188.

Tolybekov, S. Ye. *Kochevoye Obshchestvo Kazakhov, v XVII-Nachale XX veka.* Alma-Ata: "Nauka" Kazakhskoi SSR, 1971.

Tseren, P. B., "Traditional Pastoral Practice of the Oirat Mongols and Their Relationship with the Environment." In Humphrey and Sneath, eds., 1996, II: 147-159.

Tumenbayar, N. "Land Privatization in Mongolia." In .dlib. indiana.edu/documents/dir0/00/00/03/70/dlc-00000370-00/tumenbayarn041100.pdf (accessed on June 1, 2005).

Tumurjav, Myatavyn. "Traditional Animal Husbandry Techniques Practiced by Mongolian Nomadic People." In Badarch, Zilinskas, and Balint, eds., 2003: 86-113.

UB Post. "National: Underground Spokesman Explains Manhole Life." 6 December, 2004. In http://ubpost.mongolnews.mn (accessed on December 6, 2004).

World Bank. PovertyNet: Social Capital. In http://www1.worldbank.org/prem/poverty/scapital/home.htm (accessed on June 14, 2005).

Globalization's Impact on Mongolian Identity Issues and the Image of Chinggis Khan

Alicia J. Campi

PART I: The Mongols, this previously unheard-of nation that unexpectedly emerged to terrorize the whole world for two hundred years, disappeared again into obscurity with the advent of firearms. Even so, the name Mongol became one forever familiar to humankind, and the entire stretch of the thirteenth through the fifteenth centuries has come to be known as the Mongol era.[1]

PART II: The historic science was the science, which has been badly affected, and the people of Mongolia bid farewell to their history and learned by heart the history with distortion but full of ideology. Because of this, the Mongolians started to forget their religious rituals, customs and traditions and the patriotic feelings of Mongolians turned to the side of perishing as the internationalism was put above all.[2]

PART III: For decades, Mongolia had subordinated national identity to Soviet priorities....Now, they were set adrift in a sea of uncertainty, and Mongolians were determined to define themselves as a nation and as a people. The new freedom was an opportunity as well as a crisis.[3]

As the three above quotations indicate, identity issues for the Mongolian peoples have always been complicated. In our increasingly interconnected, media-driven world culture, nations with

---

[1] Baabar, *History of Mongolia* (Ulaanbaatar: Monsudar Publishing, 1999), 4.

[2] "The Political Report of the First Congress of the Mongolian Social-Democratic Party" (March 31, 1990), 14.

[3] Tsedendamdyn Batbayar, *Mongolia's Foreign Policy in the 1990s: New Identity and New Challenges* (Ulaanbaatar: Institute for Strategic Studies, 2002), 8.

small populations and histories full of difficulties in protecting national sovereignty, are both assaulted and supported by the effects of globalization. For Mongolia, the challenge of forging a new national identity under such circumstances is especially evident in 2006, when all eyes turn to Mongolia's 800th anniversary of statehood.

This anniversary commemorates the 1206 *kuriltai* that confirmed the ascendancy of Temujin over the nomadic tribal confederations by naming him khan. At this momentous 1206 assembly, Temujin took the sacred name of Chinggis, reorganized his army and administration, and chose the name *Mongol* (aka *Monggol*) for both the united tribal entity (*undes*, nationality) and associated geopolitical territory (*ulus*, nation). The mystery of the meaning of the word *Monggol* fittingly embodies the mystery surrounding exactly who and what it represented. This same ambiguity has continued through the centuries as the Mongol empire rose and waned, as the Mongol people united and split, and challenges the nation even in this globalized era.

Today Mongolia's globalization specialists are spending much time identifying priority sectors and development objectives. For example, Dr. L. Nyamtseren has noted that "for any country it is inevitable to be involved in the global process of integration. Mongolia needs to analyse carefully an [sic] international economic global trends, find out where exactly Mongolia stands at this moment, how positively or negatively the trend affects Mongolian economy and to identify its own developmental concept, strategy and policy."[4] However, in order to identify developmental strategies, economists and policy planners--Mongolian and foreign alike --first must step back and look at the issues of what is democratic Mongolia's identity should be and how integration into the globalized marketplace community will strengthen and preserve this identity.

---

4 L. Nyamtseren, "Main Developmental Pattern of Mongolia in the Edge of the 21 Century," *Renovation of Mongolia on the Eve of the XXI Century and Future Development Patterns* (Ulaanbaatar: Mongolian Development Research Center, 2000, 122-143), 140.

Although this paper will concentrate on examining the impact of globalization on establishing a modern Mongolian identity in the twenty-first century, the identity issue must first be placed within the historical context of discussion of the nature of earlier Mongolian identities. This naturally leads to an examination of the role of Mongolia's founding father, Chinggis Khan, in defining previous and present Mongolian identity issues.

CHINGGIS KHAN LINEAGE AND CULT IN THE POST-MONGOL EMPIRE PERIOD

L. Munkh-Erdene at Hokkaido University, who has researched Mongolian nationalism in the late nineteenth century to mid-1920s prior to the establishment of socialism, maintains that the prime traditional basis for Mongol statehood was the Borjigid lineage (*Mongol ovogton*) which perpetuated "the *Mongol ulus* as an historical community."[5] He cites native Mongol chronicles, which glorified Chinggis Khan and his descendants as having divine origin and the Mongol people (Blue Mongol) as the heart of an empire made up of other inferior peoples. To keep the bloodlines pure, intermarriage with the conquered Chinese people during the Yuan dynasty was prohibited. Thus, Chinggis Khan and his lineage were the cement connecting the various geographically dispersed Mongol peoples during the empire period.

In later centuries, after the breakup of the Mongol empire, lineage ties were strengthened by the fact that Chinggis Khan himself became the object of a special religious cult, centered on the Ordos region of China where a sanctuary existed housing his supposed relics.[6] In Mongolia proper, the importance of the Borjigid lin-

---

[5] Lkhamsuren Munkh-Erdene, "Inquiry to Mongolian Nationalism Through Terms and Concepts, From Late Nineteenth Century to Mid-1920s" (Sapporo, Japan: unpublished paper, 2004), 2.

[6] John Man, *Genghis Khan, Life, Death, and Resurrection* (New York: St. Martin's Press, Thomas Dunne Books, 2004), 290-298, summarizing Rihu Su, "The Chinggis Khan Mausoleum and its Guardian Tribe" (Philadelphia: University of Pennsylvania dissertation, 2000) and the April 1935 visit described in Owen Lattimore, *Mongol Journeys* (London: Doubleday, 1941).

eage continued through the Manchu Qing period (1644-1911), buttressed by a close tie to the Buddhist Church. According to Mongolian political theory, the Borjigid line was a co-ruler of the Qing Empire through alliance with, not conquest by, the Manchu royal line. Initially, Mongols during the Qing period had a policy prohibiting intermarriage with the conquered Han Chinese. Munkh-Erdene believes that when this policy finally was changed by the Manchu court in the nineteenth century, the Mongolian nobles in Urga were motivated to lead a revolution against the Qing and its successor, the Republic of China, to preserve the purity of the Mongol lineage ('one origin, one blood'). Munkh-Erdene notes that some modern Mongol researchers believe that the Mongolian noble class did have a well established *Mongol ulus* and *Mongol ovogton* identity, and were seen by the Mongol commoners (*arats* and *shabi)* as exemplifying a very different identity from the hated Manchu and Chinese officials. For all classes there was a genuine fear of Chinese cultural and physical assimilation which would lead to the disappearance of 'Mongolness'.[7]

However, Christopher Atwood does not believe the Mongols before 1911 understood the concept of nationality which is defined by customs, language and ancestry, and differs from citizenship which is defined by residence with one sovereign government.[8] Christopher Kaplonski seems to agree with Atwood because he suggests that the Mongols did not have a strong sense of ethnicity prior to the twentieth century, but rather only an identity based on "a limited locality," such as a tribe or even specific geographical location.[9] Both viewpoints are disputed by Munkh-Erdene, who maintains that during the late Qing period a new Mongol "ideology included also anti-colonial, anti-assimilation, and anti-Chinese elements…It was not and could not be a Western type of civic

---

[7] Munkh-Erdene, 2004, 3.

[8]Christopher Atwood, "National Questions and National Answers in the Chinese Revolution, Or, How Do You Say *Minzu* in Mongolian?" *East Asian Working Paper Series on Language and Politics in Modern China* 5 (Bloomington, Indiana: 1994), 37-73.

[9] Christopher Kaplonski, "Creating National Identity in Socialist Mongolia," *Central Asian Survey*, 17/1 (1998), 35-37.

nationalism."[10] Yet, Munkh-Erdene does note that perhaps with the Khiagta Agreement in 1915 there is a distinction in the way Mongols used *undesten* (nationality) for Mongols in Mongolia proper versus *ovogton* (all Mongol peoples in general). He also indicates that Jamsarano in the late 1920s refers to his 'Mongolian tribes' (*undesten*), which signifies both his nationalism and his understanding of nation.

The autonomous government under the Bogdo Khaan, a native Tibetan but spiritual and political ruler of the Mongol state which emerged from the collapse of the Qing, is a peculiar period in Mongolia's historical consciousness. During these years of turmoil and occupation by Chinese and then White Russian armies, Mongols grew in consciousness of nationhood. By this time it is clear that the Mongols had a definite sense of nationality and were seeking an independent sovereign nation for the Mongol nationality alone. This is not to say there was no idea of unification with other Mongol groups in other regions, but independence for the area of autonomous Mongolia was the major goal.

THE COMMUNIST PERIOD

After the 1921 communist revolution in Urga, power was first consolidated in the hands of the revolutionaries by the deliberate crushing of aristocratic rule. However, the arrest and execution of many in the noble class, including those claiming direct relationship to Chinggis Khan, was a peculiar problem for the new socialist government. How could the Borjigid descendants be liquidated without liquidating the Mongol state? One solution to the problem was to abolish the use of all family and clan names in 1925: "It was purely for political reasons, to eliminate the influence of the nobility and destroy the hereditary status of their children. Two or three generations later, people here didn't even know they had lost their clan names."[11] One of these people without memory

---

[10] Munkh-Erdene, 2004, 4.

[11] "In Search of Chinggis Khaan," *Mongolia Today—Online Magazine* 2 (2000), in www.mongoliatoday.com/issue/2/tomb_mistery.html.

of a clan name is N. Enkhbayar, former Prime Minister and recently elected new President of Mongolia.

During the early socialist period Mongolia needed to find a new identity, since it was tearing down its old Borjigid aristocratic one. The Mongol land had to be glorified, as well as the communist revolutionaries who had achieved independence and beaten back the foreign occupiers of the last years of the autonomous period. One major contributor to forging the new identity that was strongly linked to the physical Mongolian landscape was the poet D. Natsagdorj, who was the editor of the newspaper *A People's Warrior*. Educated in Leningrad, Berlin and Leipzig, he wrote articles about Mongolian history and the new Mongolian People's Republic (MPR) for German magazines. In 1929 he returned to Mongolia where he wrote *A Short History of Mongolia* and translated many foreign novels. In the 1930s he wrote his best dramas, including *Amidst Sad Hills*, songs, and his great poem, *My Motherland.* His works were used by the communist state to extol the new Mongolian identity: "In these poems filled with inspiration the great poet sculpted the beautiful image of Native Land dear to every Mongolian heart."[12] In fact, he was lauded as the inventor of a new genre in Mongolian literature, propaganda poems.

The conscious development of popular identification with the Mongolian land as opposed to traditional 'feudal' and religious culture is evident in Carole Pegg's research on Mongolian musical and dance genres. Pegg documents how the Mongolian official establishment in the late 1920s consciously modified old Mongolian motifs to glorify the socialist revolution, and to write out Chinggis Khan from Mongolian history and performance. Poetry and song which had been created to eulogize the founding father only could continue during the socialist period if such references were dropped. New "themes acceptable under communism included nature, the homeland, love of parents, children, the state, and the Party. References to ethnic identity and associated heroes were not permissible."[13]

---

[12]Erdenbilig (1986), 21, cited in Munkh-Erdene.

[13]Carole Pegg, *Mongolian Music, Dance, and Oral Narrative* (Seattle and London: University of Washington Press, 2001), 23.

But supporters of the traditional Borjigid lineage standard of Mongol identity did not completely disappear under communism. Mongolia's leading intellectual of the twentieth century, Biambyn Rinchen (1905-1977), was arrested in the late 1930s for being a 'nationalist', 'pan-Mongolist' and anti-revolutionary. Even after his release, he did not hide his respect for Chinggis Khan as a far-sighted world political leader. Rinchen's life motto was "Mongolia must be Mongolian," and some Mongol writers assert that he was a strong influence on the young leaders of the 1990 Mongolian democratic revolution.[14]

Meanwhile, the Japanese in the 1930s believed that they could influence communist Mongolia to move toward their camp by promoting pan-Mongolism and Chinggis Khan, following the same policy as they were pursuing in Inner Mongolia. The Mongolian leader Demid, who was accused of siding with the Japanese, was said to have proclaimed: "Let the Khalkhas return and restore the times of the Great Chingis; the Great Japan will help."[15] Under pressure from Stalin, such leaders were systematically purged from the Mongolian government.

Several decades later in 1962 Mongols sought to associate their national identification with Chinggis Khan on the 800th anniversary of his birth in Khentii aimag. A stone monument was secretly was by the government, and a conference was organized by the Academy of Sciences to assess his historical role. While the conference was in progress, a critical telegram from Soviet Academician Zhukov, who maintained Chinggis Khan had played only a 'reactionary' role in Mongolian history, was sent to B. Shirendev at the Academy. Nevertheless, some Mongol intellectuals proceeded with their favorable re-evaluation of Chinggis Khan's role. The head of the Historical Committee, Academician Natsagdorzh gave a lecture entitled "Chinggis as the Founder of the Mongol State," which was reported on by the Party newspaper *Unen.* He stressed the positive benefits Chinggis had brought to Mongolia, including

---

[14] Shagdariin Sandag and Harry H. Kendall, *Poisoned Arrows, The Stalin-Choibalsan Mongolian Massacres, 1921-1941* (Boulder: Westview Press, 2000), 149-151.

[15] Sharad K. Soni, *Mongolia-Russia Relations: Kiakhta to Vladivostok* (Delhi: Shipra Publications, 2002), 120.

unification, statehood, law codes, and literacy, versus the destructiveness of his military campaigns. Ts. Damdinsuren wrote a report refuting some of the criticism of the Soviet scholars.[16] Commemorative anniversary stamps even were issued by the government.

In September 1962 Tomor-Ochir,[17] a secretary of the Mongolian People's Revolutionary Party's Central Committee who was engaged in a political struggle with Premier Yu. Tsedenbal, was dismissed from office for inflaming nationalist feelings among the people through his connection with the Chinggis Khan anniversary. The special stamps were withdrawn and the party press criticized intellectuals who were considered too nationalistic. The whole issue was examined at a Party ideological congress in 1963, attended by a Soviet delegation under Ilichev. Robert Rupen has suggested that "probably what brought the Genghis Khan celebrations to such an abrupt end was their entanglement with the unrelated Sino-Soviet dispute, since the Chinese, viewing Genghis as an important Chinese emperor, had organized big celebrations of their own. But basically the disowning of the anniversary celebrations was a minor victory for rigidity and party solidarity in the chronic contradiction between the claims of communism and of Mongol nationalism."[18]

The legacy of the failed attempt to resurrect Chinggis Khan is seen by the fact that ten years later, noted Mongolian historians Shirendev, Natsagdorzh, Perlee, and Bira in their *History of the Mongolian People's Republic* criticized Chinese historians for being "apologists for Genghis Khan and his bloodthirsty deeds."[19] They quoted Tsedenbal and the January 1963 report by B. Lkhamsuren at the Republican Conference on Problems of Ideological Work.

---

[16]D. Dashpurev and S.K. Soni, *Reign of Terror in Mongolia 1920-1990* (New Delhi: South Asian Publishers, 1992), 61-62.

[17] Tomor-Ochir is thought to have been killed in 1985 by pro-Tsendenbal supporters with the help of the Mongolian secret police, the *Dotood Yam*. See Dashpurev (1992), 63 and 76 n. 30.

[18]C.R. Bawden, *The Modern History of Mongolia* (New York: Frederick A. Praeger, 1968), 418-419.

[19]*History of the Mongolian People's Republic* (Moscow: Nauka Publishing House, 1973), 54.

The official history admitted that there was some progressive significance to Chinggis Khan organizing the tribes in a single organic state, yet cautioned that "attention must be drawn to the quite obviously ruinous effects of the Genghis Khan conquests both on the peoples who were subdued and on Mongolia itself, the population of which was reduced and its productive forces dispersed over foreign lands."[20]

The anti-Chinggis Khan line and dissociation of the founding father with the Mongol state continued to be maintained by the Mongolian government and intellectual establishment until the end of the socialist period. This was explained in the official history as: "The political unification of Mongolia in a single state could have helped towards a further advance in the country's productive resources and its economic and cultural progress. The obstacle to this, however, was the aggressive policy of the Mongol feudal leaders headed by Genghis Khan, who turned the people into warriors and the country into a military camp. The aggressive campaigns of Genghis Khan and his successors against the peoples of China, Iran, Russia and other countries were a supreme disaster, since they held up for a long time the progressive development of those peoples. During these campaigns enormous material and cultural assets were destroyed and tens of thousands of people were wiped out. The aggressive wars of the Mongol feudal leaders also had the effect of halting the growth of the productive forces and culture of Mongolia itself and brought the Mongolian people nothing but sufferings."[21]

THE REVIVAL OF CHINGGIS KHAN DURING THE DEMOCRATIC REVOLUTION

In the 1989-1990 struggle by the young Mongolian democrats against communism, the leading political parties put forth a number of demands, one of which focused on Mongolian identity issues. They called for "the revival of traditional Mongolian culture,

[20] *History of MPR* (1973), 54 and 518 n. 120.

[21] *Ibid.*, 13.

re-introduction of the old Mongolian script, rehabilitation of Genghis Khan and encouragement to Buddhism."[22] The founding father of Mongolia, dead 800 years, suddenly was pulled from the rubbish heap of history by young, historically ignorant Mongols seeking both to criticize their communist elders and find a new nationalistic identity. Rock musicians sang songs dedicated to the Great Khan. The nation's number one band, Khonkh, stood next to a giant portrait of Chinggis and mournfully sang an apologia for the lack of respect of previous generations: "Will you forgive us?/ For we used to focus/Only on the black spots of your life,/Distorting the record of history/And thus deceiving future generations."[23] The term Bogdo Ezhen [saintly/holy/august Lord/Ruler] was found increasingly in opposition political newspapers and documents.[24]

This phenomenon was certainly initially home-grown. Mongol writers such as Sh. Sandag, when reviewing the communist past, have claimed that one of the main reasons Mongolia maintained its independence during the twentieth century was because any country that produced such great world leaders as Chinggis Khan and Khubilai Khan could not have its statehood and cultural identity extinguished.[25]

In early 1990, prior to the downfall of the communist government, an organization called the "Palace of Chinggis Khan," which was meant to represent the *ovogton* or large extended family descended from the world conqueror, was established by Khalkha Mongols claiming direct descent from him. This private social and cultural association was given much publicity in official and non-official newspapers as having the goal of the perpetuation of the memory of Chinggis. Yet the organization was open to all Mongols regardless of bloodlines, because Chinggis Khan is the father of Mongolia and thus the ancestor of all Mongols. At this time

---

[22] Soni, 2002, 223, quoting Mike Faber, "Mongolia Moves Towards Perestroika," *Development Policy Review* 8:4 (December 1990), 426.
[23] Nicholas Kristof, "Where Genghis Khan Is In," *The New York Times Magazine* (May 27, 1990), 23.
[24] *Ardchilal* [Democracy] 7 (June 1-10, 1990), 4.
[25] Sandag and Kendall, 2000, 170.

daily prayers with incense in his honor were resumed after a more than a sixty year hiatus at the capital's Gandan monastery.

The Mongolian Revolutionary People's Party (MPRP), in the midst of rejecting communism and reincarnating itself as a social democratic party, faced a national election in 1990, and thus desired to identify with the growing nationalistic movement praising the great khan. It permitted a modest public celebration in honor of Chinggis Khan's birthday in May with a special edition of the newspaper *Unen*, full of articles on Chinggis, including an article by an astrologer which concluded that the Mongol leader conveniently was born on May 1st (traditional communist May Day could then be retained as a national holiday). The newspaper also included the text of the poem, "The Tomb of Chinggis," composed by national poet R. Choinom in the early 1960s but until then banned from print as too chauvinistic and nationalistic.

The nationalistic frenzy was fed by the events surrounding the conference held in Ulaanbaatar in August 1990 dedicated to the 750th anniversary of the *Secret History of the Mongols*. Although planning for the event had started years before and the Mongolian government had obtained UNESCO support to celebrate the anniversary of the writing of this unique Mongolian historical epic about Chinggis Khan's life, only small announcements were placed in *Unen* explaining the conference. A nine-part stamp series, with only one stamp of Chinggis' image, was printed. However, the winds of political reform and revived Mongolian nationalism encouraged the conference's activists and young scholars to glorify the nation's founder. Quickly, a new ballet for children and an opera were commissioned, and special songs and poems were written.

A special exhibit devoted exclusively to works glorifying Chinggis Khan was organized by the Mongolian Artists Union, timed to correspond with the conference on the *Secret History*. In a pan-Mongolist gesture, art pieces also were displayed from well-known Inner Mongolian artists. Images of Chinggis Khan proliferated in the 'black market' and portraits bearing his injunction: "If my body dies, let it die, but do not let my country die," appeared everywhere. Also, there was an artistic movement to modify the Chinese-stylized official Yuan dynastic portrait characterization of

Chinggis to make him appear less sinicized, younger, and more Mongol in physical appearance. Thus, the 1990 Secret History conference became for Mongols the catalyst for an explosion of long suppressed joy and pride over Chinggis Khan.

With the Democratic Revolution, Mongols were able to focus not only on redefining national identity, but also on restoring their own personal tribal and family identities. In 1991 President P. Ochirbat began the process with a decree restoring family names. People were permitted to choose their own name, and over sixty percent chose the name of the clan of Chinggis, the *Mongol ovogton*, Borjigid.[26] This was an indication of the strong identification Mongols continued to have to a common ancestor or common bone that is connected to the Borjigid royal lineage.

EXPOSURE TO GLOBALIZATION NURTURES TRADITIONAL IDENTITY THEMES

Newly democratic Mongolia in the 1990s was exposed to the modern Western world and the whole issue of globalization. At first glance, it might be assumed that globalization's impact on modern Mongolia's identity only would favor the emerging urban culture over the traditional rural one, accelerating the evolutionary process from the socialist era. Connecting Mongolia with the technologically diverse Western world with its instant media seemingly should promote the new over the old in the minds of its people. In fact, concern has grown that Mongolia in this new global era is losing its traditional culture or is a society split in two, as the modern urban Western lifestyle centered around Ulaanbaatar loses touch with the needs of the growing poor rural herdsmen around the country.

Many Mongols inside and outside the government were forced to re-examine the question of "what is Mongolia's identity?" The government's particular challenge is to formulate development strategies for Mongolia that maintain Mongolia's uniqueness and sovereignty, as the nation seeks to integrate itself more within the

[26] "In Search," 2003.

Asian region, something that its long-standing Soviet ties had prevented for over seventy years. Coming up with a modern reformulation of Mongolia's identity in today's globalized world is an issue that has been discussed for the last fifteen years by Mongolia's policymakers and strategic studies experts. For example, Tsedendambyn Batbayar from the Institute of Strategic Studies has written extensively on Mongolia's search for a new post-Soviet identity. Noting that early Mongolian nationalism was submerged beneath the expansive push of both China and Russia, he claimed that in 1990 "independence rekindled the desire to rediscover Mongolian identity."[27] For Batbayar, Mongolia's identity must be a product of geography, of culture which includes Chinggis Khan, and of foreign policy. He believes that as Mongolia debates whether it belongs to Central Asia or Northeast Asia, it is actually debating if it will have a nomadic versus a modern identity.

Batbayar and many other Mongolian policymakers have an obvious bias against nomadism, implying that if Mongolia retains traditional nomadism, it cannot become modern. Thus they reject the nomadic economic model which has sustained the nation and people in difficult climatic and geographical conditions over the centuries. Most of the Western development and poverty alleviation experts who advise Mongolia promote such a biased, dismissive attitude, as seen in UNDP and Asian Development Bank reports. The embodiment of rejecting nomadism is Mongolian President Enkhbayar, who when prime minister famously stated: "It is not my desire to destroy the original Mongolian identity but in order to survive we have to stop being nomads."[28]

However, some Mongolian economists, such as D. Byambasuren, are convinced that nomadism is one of the keys to Mongolian modern as well as traditional identity: "In the history of [sic] world, Mongols are known as nomadic herders, bearing the nomadic branch of traditional civilization tree at the edge of the twentieth century. Therefore, nomadic life values and culture are to appear as a main basis that determine national mentality and ways

---

27 Batbayar, 2002, 17.

28 David Murphy, "No Room for Nomads," *Far Eastern Economic Review* (May 31, 2001), 122.

of survival of Mongols."[29] Some modern Mongolian anthropologists believe that Mongolian nomads are freedom loving, individualistic, and quick learners, characteristics highly suitable to the new democratic free market era.

Like the communists of the last century, modern Mongolian policymakers today have the dilemma of choosing what in traditional Mongolian culture to promote and what to denigrate and change. The Mongolian nomadic lifestyle and economy with its special form of poverty dramatically increased in the country's early globalization period, so it is debatable whether or not nomadism is destined in fact to disappear. In the early twenty-first century, it is apparent that the majority of Mongolia's leaders choose to reject nomadism as a backward economic form despite its being uniquely Mongolian, but they still seek to retain and glorify the national father of Mongolian nomadism, Chinggis Khan. They can take this attitude because, curiously, in the democratic era the Mongols have found that many Westerners actually highly respect Chinggis Khan for his empire rather than criticize him as 'uncivilized'.

WESTERN VIEWS OF CHINGGIS KHAN INFLUENCE DEMOCRATIC MONGOLIA'S IMAGE

Globalization's impact of linking Mongolia to international cultural and ecological non-governmental organizations (NGOs), such as affiliates of the United Nations like UNESCO and ecological/environmental groups, somewhat unexpectedly is providing financial underwriters and vocal advocates for preserving traditional Mongolian cultural elements which had been under attack for so much of the socialist twentieth century. Living between two giant neighbors which had little affection or nostalgia for the Mongolian empire, the Mongols had become accustomed to foreigners negatively evaluating their historical past. However, with the end

---

[29]D. Byambasuren, "National Factors Affecting Development Strategy of Mongolia," *Renovation of Mongolia on the Eve of the XXI Century and Future Development Patterns* (Ulaanbaatar: Mongolian Development Research Center, 2000), 107.

of Mongolia's isolation from the global marketplace in the 1990s, some Western nations, particularly the United States, Canada, Australia, and Great Britain which were not overrun by the Mongols and did not have any memory of destruction or murder to color their views, indicated they were favorably impressed by what they knew of Chinggis Khan and his empire. Mongolia soon clearly understood that the one thing almost everyone in the world did know about the country was Chinggis Khan, and for many of these foreigners he was awe-inspiring rather than awful. As Nicholas Kristof of *The New York Times* wrote: "He may have killed people by the millions, but he was also a great nationalist and one of the most brilliant commanders in history."[30]

Mongols also learned that many serious Mongolists in the United States wrote with admiration about Chinggis Khan. For example, Kaplonski asserted that "Genghis Khan forged the Mongols into a unified group of people and created a nation single-handedly. He's like George Washington and Abraham Lincoln and all our Founding Fathers rolled into one."[31] There was even the radical approach to Chinggis Khan, advanced by Paula Sabloff, which has led to a new school of reinterpreting him as a democratic leader.[32] Even a scientifically-trained Mongolian historian such as Batbayar was enthralled by the peculiar concept that his nation's once despised founder is not associated just with murder, but also with promoting democratic principles![33] Thus, many in the Mongolian intellectual and political establishment have enthusiastically embraced Chinggis Khan not only as a symbol of past glories, but also as a symbol recognized around the world as a great leader of the new democratic Mongolia.

But why were Westerners in the 1990s attracted to Chinggis Khan and the imperial past in the "democratic" Mongolia? The founding father, who had been a non-person for much of the twentieth century, became the object of intense foreign curiosity

---

30 Kristof, 1990, 23.

31 Beth Brophy, "Rethinking the Legendary Barbarian Genghis Khan," in *Untold Tales of the Great Conquerors*. U.S. New and World Report (2005), 48.

32 Paula Sabloff, *Modern Mongolia: Reclaiming Genghis Khan* (Philadelphia: University of Pennsylvania Museum of Archaeology and Anthropology, 2001).

33 Batbayar, 2002, 26.

when the young Mongolian anti-communists used his image in their demonstrations as a nationalistic rallying point. Foreigners then sought to "sell" Chinggis Khan by linking his name to their efforts and products to attract the favor of the Mongols. The first major manifestation of this phenomenon was the "Gurvan Gol" ['Three Rivers'] expedition conducted by a group of Japanese scientists and Mongolian Academy of Sciences from 1990 to 1993, sponsored by the *Yomiuri Shimbun* newspaper. Japanese scientists employed ultrasound technology to identify as many as 1380 underground cavities that could be old royal tombs. However, the expedition was very controversial from the outset, because the Japanese were accused of bribing Mongolian officials to secretly prospect for minerals under the cover of searching for Chinggis Khan's tomb. The expedition had not counted on the intense protests of the Mongolian public against any attempt to excavate for the grave, because of the taboo about desecrating the burial spot Chinggis had made such a great attempt to hide from the world.

As we approach the 800th anniversary of Mongolian statehood, we are now in the midst of an ever greater Chinggis Khan boom promoted by foreigners. The origin can be traced to a 1995 article in *The Washington Post* which named the Mongolian leader the "Man of the Millennium."[34] After Sabloff's promotion of Chinggis Khan as a democratic leader worthy of modern Mongolia, a number of new biographies by non-Mongolist writers such as Jack Weatherford[35] of MacCalester College and John Man[36] of Great Britain appeared to great sales. Weatherford, whose well-written book reached *The New York Times* bestseller list despite its shaky scholarship, has been interviewed on National Public Radio and other programs in the United States to explain his view that Chinggis Khan was a progressive, wrongly criticized, great ruler.[37]

---

[34] Joel Achenbach, "The Era of His Ways," *The Washington Post* (December 31, 1995), F1.

[35] Jack Weatherford, *Genghis Khan and the Making of the Modern World* (New York: Crown Press), 2004.

[36] John Man, *Genghis Khan, Life, Death, and Resurrection* (New York: St. Martin's Press, 2004).

[37] "All Things Considered," National Public Radio, with Robert Siegel, March 25, 2004, in http://www.npr.org/templates/story/story.php?storyId=1791972.

Chinggis Khan has attracted the attention of other types of media: the BBC has a one-hour documentary planned for release in 2005-6; Russian director Sergey Bodrov is planning a Hollywood-style epic on the young Chinggis called "The Mongol;" and there also is a much hyped film project on Chinggis Khan announced by Hollywood actor Steven Segal.

U.S. News and World Report in the fall of 2005 published a collector's edition on "Untold Tales of the Great Conquerors," which has an article on rethinking Chinggis Khan's legacy. It concludes that perhaps Chinggis was both a barbarian and a renaissance man: "Now, nearly eight centuries after his death, Genghis Khan's reputation seems to be undergoing a dream makeover."[38] British reporter Andrew Osborn has written that Chinggis Khan, modern Mongolia's sole historical figure capable of resurrecting a sense of greatness, is a "feel-good rallying point," for a people increasingly disenchanted with the country's supposedly democratic post-Communist rulers.[39] Even foreign-organized adventure tourists, newly exposed to Mongolia in this globally-interconnected world are encouraged to go to Mongolia to view the new Chinggis Khan as no barbarian, but "a pragmatic assimilationist," whose legacy to his nation was "the curious, hungry readiness to embrace good things from whatever sources and to combine them opportunistically as life flows along."[40] Is this not a recipe for success for the modern globalization proponent?

The foreigners' dream to find the tomb of Chinggis Khan has not gone away. For several years there has been an American expedition pressuring Mongolian officials for permission to survey likely sites, and in 2005 this search has even been turned into a kind of archaeological tourism. It seems step by step the world-wide media (e.g. *National Geographic*, the History and Discovery channels, the *Wall Street Journal*, *International Herald Tribune*, *Time Magazine*), manipulated by foreigners seeking tomb booty and/or

---

[38] Beth Brophy, "Rethinking the Legendary Barbarian Genghis Khan," in *Untold Tales of the Great Conquerors.* U.S. New and World Report (2005), 46-51.

[39] Andrew Osborn, "The Cult of Genghis Khan," *Independent News* (London: May 11, 2005).

[40] David Quammen, "In the Kingdom of Eternal Blue Heaven," *National Geographic Adventure* (January 2006),102.

international fame, are complicit in pressing the Mongolian authorities to agree to search for the founding father's burial site.

Even if Chinggis Khan is not considered a democratic national leader, it is clear that most of Mongolia's contemporary historians as well as the populace would agree with Mongolian historian Baabar who wrote about Chinggis and his meaning for today's Mongols: "For Mongols who traditionally revered their ancestors, Chinggis Khaan was a god….Chinggis Khaan is something more than [a national hero] for Mongols: their lodestar, spiritual force, and the object of not only of national but of personal pride."[41]

However, there is a small caveat: below the surface, such adoration of Chinggis Khan as the symbol of "Mongolness" recently seems to be producing a murmuring backlash. This author has spoken with Western-educated young Mongolian intellectuals who decry the national fixation and glorification of the great khan. Perhaps they are responding to the obvious clash between exalting the founding father and denigrating the traditional nomadic culture which he epitomizes. It appears that this contradiction will continue to pull at the Mongolian psyche, and globalization and integration into the world perhaps exacerbate, not resolve, this issue.

INNER MONGOLIAN IDENTITY ISSUES

Among other Mongol peoples physically outside the independent nation, the search for national identity in our newly interconnected world is similarly tortured and contorted. There are several young Inner Mongolian scholars who have been confronting the question of "Who are the Mongols?" in the multi-ethnic state of modern China.

One such scholar is Almaz Khan, who from Berkeley has written on the *minzu* identity of the Mongols at the end of the twentieth century. He notes that the Mongolian identity is a matter of negotiation and contestation between the Mongols and the Han Chinese as well as between different regional and occupational

---

[41] Baabar, 1999, 34.

subgroups of Mongols in Inner Mongolia. He calls this complex web of relationships which affect the overall Mongol group identity "a homogenizing 'Mongolness' for the *public* domain."[42] Khan emphasizes the importance of historical memory on the part of Mongols and Chinese in Mongolian "self-imaging and representation."[43] Both ethnic groups focus on the 'otherness' of Mongolian identity. Mongolia is beautiful, wild, mysterious, barbaric, and dangerous. Such an image affects the "PRC state politico-economic policy and practice and has affected the process and shape of the Mongol's *minzu* identity." Despite the fact that millions of Chinese agriculturalists for over a century have poured into the Inner Mongolian territory and this massive colonization has changed the traditional pastoral economy and demography and forced most Mongols to give up animal husbandry to adopt agriculture and urban living, *Nei Menggu* [Inner Mongolia] "continues to be perceived the way it has always been: as an exotic and wild region where all is boundless blue sky, grassland, herds, and nomads."[44]

Khan asserts that this archaic image of the pastoral Inner Mongolia has been propagated since the founding of the People's Republic of China through the spread of state media and arts, especially by television. Nevertheless, Han Chinese sociopolitical control in the latter half of the twentieth century has advocated the "advanced" state of a settled way of life and forced more and more Mongols to shift away from pastoral life to agriculture. This then has accelerated the disintegration of a coherent Mongolian culture and society, which in turn "has served to awaken a stronger sense of Mongol ethnic consciousness and a keenly felt need for, and attempts at, cultural revival and identity reinforcement. This reinforcement centers on the symbolism of pastoralism in opposition to the agricultural."[45]

The oppression of the Cultural Revolution in Inner Mongolia inspired an ethnic revival movement in the 1980s, yet since the

---

42 Almaz Khan, "Who Are the Mongols? State, Ethnicity, and the Politics of Representation in the PRC," in Melissa J Brown, ed., *Negotiating Ethnicities in China and Taiwan* (Berkeley: Institute of East Asian Studies, 1996), 126.

43 *Ibid.*, 127.

44 *Ibid.*, 132.

45 *Ibid.*, 139.

Cultural Revolution most Mongols no longer wear traditional dress and urban Mongols generally are unable to speak Mongolian. Mongolian political representation in the regional government has dropped from 50 percent in 1947 to 10-15 percent in the new century. In response to the real issue of ethnic survival, Khan recognizes the growth of art and literature, often associated with Chinggis Khan, to express Mongolian sentiments, and the emphasis on the image of pastoralism as a rallying point, cultural marker and demarcation of Mongolian identity.[46] "For the Inner Mongols, Chinggis Khan has come to serve specifically as a symbol of ethnic/cultural survival of their group in relation to the overwhelmingly dominant Chinese state and society."[47] Yet, for the wealthier, more politically facile Inner Mongolian intellectuals and urban Mongols, the embracing of the pastoral symbols to which they attach sentimental value but do not represent their actual everyday Chinese way of life reality is a kind of "self-denial" of their actual cultural lives or "self-othering."[48] Such Mongols are the majority, and they usually are embarrassed by their rural cousins, but as agriculturalists and city-dwellers who have "demographic and economic weight, they have no (positive) symbolic values to offer to the nation-state, the Han Chinese, or the Mongols as a whole."[49]

Inner Mongolia's attitudes toward Chinggis Khan, according to Khan, are different from how 'Outer Mongols' see him. Khan believes that Chinggis Khan as a national symbol was suppressed in the nation of Mongolia during the communist period not because he was a rival rallying point of Mongolian nationalism, but for political reasons governed by the Sino-Soviet relationship and because the Russians never liked the Mongol conqueror.[50] Khan explains that Chinggis Khan became "a symbol of opposition and yearning for a strong Mongol fatherland and independent nation-

---

46 *Ibid.*, 143.

47 Almaz Khan, "Chinggis Khan: From Imperial Ancestor to Ethnic Hero," in Stevan Harrell, ed., *Cultural Encounters on China's Ethnic Frontiers* (Seattle ; London: University of Washington Press, 1995), 248.

48 Khan, "Who?," 1996, 152.

49 *Ibid.*, 154.

50 *Ibid.*, 262.

state,"[51] so democratic Mongolia rightly has elevated him to a national hero.

Uradyn Bulag, who has established himself as an expert on Chinese Mongolian minority policies, also has written about the Chinese 'Inner' Mongols quest for identity through Chinggis Khan: "What Mongols see of themselves in assessing the twentieth century is that they are weak and overwhelmed by the Chinese, and that they are themselves hopelessly divided, unable to either become a united people or defend their interests in the face of the combination of a powerful Chinese state and large-scale Chinese migration to Inner Mongolia. Their decline in this century is a sharp contrast to their history of glory and valor. The constant yearning for Chinggis Khan is, in this sense, a yearning for the recovery of Mongol prowess."[52]

Bulag has noted that the Chinese cleverly appropriated Chinggis Khan in the twentieth century and made him a Chinese hero--"the only Chinese to defeat the Europeans." Bulag sees this as a revision of Chinese multiculturalism theory, so that Mongolian and other non-Han Chinese heroes, who were long denounced as China's enemies, are now defined as Chinese.[53] Yet, how Han nationalism, which was originally targeted against China's historical enemies such as the Mongols and Manchus, could then embrace unwilling non-Han peoples as equals in the post-dynastic period, becomes a real question.

China's absorption of Mongolia's founding hero has been a centuries-long process. The Manchu Qing dynasty created a special administrative unit supported by an annual budget to care for the shrine of Chinggis Khan in the Ordos. In the nineteenth century the Qing court opened Inner Mongolian grasslands to Chinese agricultural development and settlement. After the establishment of the Republic of China in 1911, Inner Mongols experienced even more intense Chinese colonialism which in the main erased

---

[51] *Ibid.*, 263.

[52] Uradyn E. Bulag, *The Mongols at China's Edge: History and the Politics of National Unity* (Lanham: Rowman & Littlefield, 2002), 234-235.

[53] Uradyn E. Bulag, "The Chinese Cult of Chinggis Khan: Genealogical Nationalism and Problems of National and Cultural Integrity" (Victoria, Canada; October 3-5, 2003), 2.

Inner Mongolia as a viable independent political entity. The cult and symbolism of Chinggis Khan lost its dynastic sponsorship. Meanwhile, in independent communist Mongolia, after the late 1920s, the Chinggis Khan cult was suppressed and local shrines destroyed.

When the Japanese established control in Manchuria in the 1930s under the Manchukuo government, they planned to permanently house the Ordos relics and memorial to Chinggis Khan in a massive mausoleum in Ulaanhot, Inner Mongolia to rally the Mongolian tribes to their side in the fight to expand Japan's Greater Co-Prosperity Sphere. Mongols, supported by Pu Yi's Daur (Darhad) Mongol wife Wan Rong and the Daur general Guo Wenling, built a Chinggis Khan temple (completed on September 30, 1943), the central symbol of Mongolian nationalism in eastern Inner Mongolia. This temple, Wang Yeh Miao, was "where the guardian spirit of the holy founder of the Mongol dynasty will be deeply revered, so that it may become a shining example for the creation of a united Great Asia."[54]

However, pro-Chinese Nationalist princes appealed to the Nationalist army to protect the Ordos relics from removal. As a result, they were evacuated to Gansu and passed through Communist-held Yenan to a welcome by a 10,000-strong throng. In 1944 the Communists with Mao's approval established a Chinggis Khan memorial with statue in Yenan. When the Communists won the Chinese civil war, their new government, to placate the Inner Mongols, constructed a large Chinggis Khan mausoleum in 1954, remarkably similar in design to the destroyed Japanese model. It consisted of three *ger*-shaped buildings at Ejin Horoo Banner in the Ordos for the housing of treasures and 'relics'. There, the Darkhad guardians of the sanctuary were confirmed in their positions and the Chinese government subsidized annual sacrifices.[55] It officially was dedicated on April 8, 1956, the year of the Sino-Soviet split, so Chinese officials also may have been trying to woo the goodwill of the Mongols across the border.[56]

---

54 "Genghis Khan's New Fan Club," *The London Times* (June 1, 1980).
55 Bawden, 1968, 417.
56 "Genghis Khan's," 1980.

The present Inner Mongolian autonomous region took shape only in 1956, at a time when Mongols were already a 1-5 minority in their own homeland. For Inner Mongols, especially communist ones, there still is a continuous struggle to resolve the nationality question of how historical and cultural differences between Mongols and Chinese are mediated in a socialist, but nationalist, regime.[57] Khan sees a parallel evolution in the evolving of Chinggis Khan from an exclusive symbol of imperial legitimacy through actual kinship bloodlines to an embracing symbol of ancestry for all Mongols (all are "sons and grandsons of Chinggis Khan," as Mao said).[58] He also attributes the growth of the image of Chinggis Khan to mass media and Chinese movies. It will be interesting to watch as China opens itself up to globalization to see how the world's fascination and reinterpretation of Chinggis Khan will impact on both Han Chinese marketing strategy and theory of China as a multi-ethnic culture.

Complicating the identity situation is the reaction of Han Chinese to Chinggis Khan in communist China. Wurlig Borchigud, a researcher who claims direct descent from Chinggis Khan's Borjigid clan, has written about how China used its educational system in the 1950s and 1960s to formulate a common Chinese culture of shared descent by teaching that all modern Chinese ethnic groups, including the Inner Mongols, are natives of China's common territory and actually can trace their origins to the founding Yellow Emperor of China.[59] After the destruction of the Cultural Revolution was repaired, Chinese since the 1980s have been flocking to the Ordos shrine of Chinggis Khan to 'worship' him as a Chinese national hero. To Bulag such a phenomenon serves the interest of contemporary Chinese nationalism: "The Chinese cult of Chinggis Khan may be understood both as a statist attempt to accommodate minorities within China and as the exercise of a racial nat-i-

---

[57] Bulag, 2002, 7.

[58] The Yunnan Mongol community published a poem entitled, "We Are the Sons and Daughters of the Steppes: Children and Grandchildren of Chinggis Khan," Khan, "Chinggis", 275-276.

[59]Wurlig Borchigud, "The Impact of Urban Ethnic Education on Modern Mongolian Ethnicity, 1949-1966," in Stevan Harrell, ed., *Cultural Encounters on China's Ethnic Frontiers* (Seattle ; London: University of Washington Press, 1995), 279.

onalism on the part of a victimized nation seeking to exact revenge for the humiliations of Euro-American and Japanese colonialisms of the nineteenth and twentieth centuries."[60]

How then have the Inner Mongols reacted to all of this? Have the Mongols in China taken pride in the Chinese embrace of their national hero? A measure of the tension between Chinese and Inner Mongolian views of national identity as seen through the prism of Chinggis Khan is played out today over the plan for the government of China to spend about $20 million to renovate the Ordos mausoleum shrine built to Chinggis Khan. A local but well-connected Han Chinese businessman has proposed revamping the shrine into an entertainment complex and theme park, attractive to domestic and foreign tourists. Chinggis Khan would be packaged by the Chinese as the founder of a great Chinese dynasty and a good tourist attraction in his own right. The shrine would be privatized and its maintenance taken away from the Darkhad Mongol traditional protectors to become a profitable Chinese Mongolian Disneyland! Inner Mongolian authorities in 2004 quietly had agreed to let construction begin on the new project.

However, press accounts were published revealing the construction plans. News spread quickly among the 3.9 million ethnic Mongols in Inner Mongolia. In late 2004 campuses of the Inner Mongolian Normal University and other universities had to be sealed off, and a concert by the famous hard rock band from independent Mongolia, Hurd, was cancelled to stave off demonstrations.[61] Darkhad Mongol pickets gathered at the mausoleum site for over a month, forcing the local government in December 2004 to halt construction and sack the mausoleum/museum director. The sensitive issue, described on internet sites, has mobilized the Inner Mongols and Mongols outside China to resist further attempts at commercializing the shrine: "This shrine is ours. The state doesn't own them [relics]--we do."[62]

---

[60] *Ibid.*, 2-3.

[61] James Brooks, "Ulan Bator Journal: The Mongolians Are Coming to China With Heavy Metal! China Frets Over Mongolian Metal Band," *The New York Times* (November 26, 2004).

[62] B. Gardi, "In Inner Mongolia, Tribe Resists Bid to Turn Shrine Into a Theme Park," *Radio Free Asia* (February 17, 2005), in www.smhric.org/news-75.htm.

It is a good guess that the whole question of how to treat Chinggis Khan and his importance in identity issues, for both Han Chinese and Inner Mongols, will continue to be a significant issue. Khan concludes that "the symbolism of Chinggis Khan has gone through a complicated history of change in signification and application," and shown a high degree of adaptability in different historical contexts as the concept of Mongolian ethnicity in China has changed.[63]

SOME COMMENTS ON THE KALMYK AND BURIAT MONGOLIAN IDENTITIES

For Mongol groups still incorporated in the Russian state after the collapse of socialism in 1990, a re-examination of national identity issues, particularly when exposed to the successful independence movements in the Baltic and Central Asian republics, naturally took place. Buriats were annexed to the Russian state in treaties in 1689 and 1728, when the territories on both sides of Lake Baikal were separated from what is now independent Mongolia. From that time until the early twentieth century, the Buriat population increased from 27,700 to 300,000. Buriats to the west of Baikal (Irkutsk Buriats) were Christianized, 'russified', and took up sedentary agriculture. The eastern Buriats (Transbaikal Buriats) remained Lamaist Buddhists and some continued to be *ger*-dwelling. Under the Czarist government, Buddhism thrived and became an important factor in Buriat cultural development, as it was among the Khalkhas to the south. The Buddhist Church ceased to exist officially in the 1930s, during the Stalinist general persecution of religion. In 1958 the word 'Mongol' was removed from the name of the republic (Buriat ASSR).

However, in the late 1980s there was a revival of lamaism as part of Buriat Mongol national consolidation and spiritual rebirth.[64] Contacts between Buriats and independent Mongolia increased greatly during the democratic era. While certainly having an

---

63 Khan, "Chinggis," 277.

64 www.economicexpert.com/a/buryat.htm.

opportunity to learn more about the father of the Mongolian nation, Chinggis Khan, was one of the results of communication with other Mongol groups and Western nations, Buriat national identity also was influenced by the revival of shamanism. Perhaps renewal of shamanic practices was accepted as part of the revival of traditional 'Russian' forms of religious practices (which also included Lamaism), and thus was more acceptable to Russian political authorities, who feared any 'pan-Mongolism' movement.

Research on this intriguing topic is being done by doctoral student Manduhai at Harvard University, who did two years of field work among Buriats in Dornod, Mongolia and at the Ulaanbaatar Shamanic Center. She argues that "one of the multiple meanings of Buriat shamanic practices is a construction of nationalism--as an imagined community that articulates a collective identity. Shamans foster nationalism by bringing together the spirits of lost land, Buriat people, and the Celestial Court in one communal ritual. Research shows that such practice of nationalism was developed historically as a form of Buriat resistance to colonialism and displacement."[65] Manduhai concludes that the political instability within Mongolia led to shamanism's resurgence among Mongol Buriats.

As for the Kalmyk Mongols, this semi-nomadic branch of the Oirat Mongols migrated from Chinese Turkistan to the steppe west of the Volga in the mid-seventeenth century. As allies of the Russians, they guarded the eastern frontier of the Russian Empire for Peter the Great. About 300,000 Kalmyks who lived east of the Volga in 1771 tried to return to China but were tragically decimated enroute. The Kalmyks west of the Volga, who remained in Russia as practicing Lamaists, were given the Turkish name Kalmyk or 'remnant'. After the incorporation of the Soviet Union, the Kalmyks were given an autonomous region. However, many Kalmyk units fought the Russians in collaboration with the Nazi Germans in World War II, so Stalin deported about 170,000 to Siberia in 1943 and dissolved their republic. About 6,000 were all-

---

[65] Buyandelgeriyn Manduhai, "The Spirit of My Homeland is Recalling Me: Nationalism, Landscape, and Ritual Among the Buriats of Mongolia: Abstract," Central Eurasian Studies Society 4th Annual Conference (Boston, October 2003).

owed to return to the Volga homeland under Khrushchev and the Kalmyk ASSR was re-established in 1958.

The Kalmyks sought independence at the dissolution of the USSR in the 1990s, but instead were made a republic within the Russian Federation in February 1992 in an effort to calm the political crisis. The new president of the republic agreed to abandon their separatist claims in 1994. In the post-Soviet period, Kalmyk Buddhism and cultural forms such as the Kalmyk epic Janggar have been revived. Still, the Mongolness of the Kalmyks is proclaimed on the official website of the republic, where reference is made to the fact that the Kalmyks "used to be a part of the Mongol state created by Chenghis-khan in the 13th century." It also defines the Kalmyks as "a Mongol-speaking nation in the European part of Russia."[66]

CONCLUSION

Mongolia is trying to establish itself as a viable democratic, Western-oriented, free market economy with a unique and valuable native culture. It is seeking to redefine its national identity and world image in terms that inspire its own people and at the same time revise any negative image left from its imperial past 800 years ago. "Mongols are seeing off the 20th century with the crisis of ethical heritage."[67] The key to this search for a new identity appears to be the redefining and renewal of the symbol of Chinggis Khan, the founder of both the Mongolian state and nationality. As the historian Baabar told a foreign reporter in 2005: "He is the founder of our state, the root of our history. The communists very brutally cut us off from our traditions and history and got us to adopt the ways and views of Western civilization--with a red color of course, but still Western. Now we are becoming Mongols again."[68]

---

66 www.kalmykykiaembassy.ru/html/ehistory/html.

67 Byambasuren (2000), 109.

68 Pocha, "Mongolia" (2005).

Byambasuren proclaims that at this period of new independence after the struggles of the twentieth century, it is not wrong to be proud of the great Mongol empire. He maintains that the only way Mongolia can progress in the world is if Mongols themselves are healthy: "True essence of this phenomenon is that Mongols discovered themselves in a completely new way and started to restore their national values."[69] Dr. Ts. Tsetsenbileg of the Mongolian Academy of Sciences notes that "understanding how Mongolians view Genghis Khan throws light on how Mongolians view their own heritage and, to a certain extent, themselves. Within this rapidly changing world, Genghis Khan, if we acknowledge him without bias, can service as a moral anchor. He can be Mongolia's root, its source of certainty at a time when many things are uncertain."[70]

Most of the international response to this emerging Mongolian identity has been positive. Mongols are no longer feared nor looked down upon as barbarians. In fact, foreigners have reacted very enthusiastically to preserving Mongolian culture and history which has permitted the Mongols, regardless of where they live, to explore their roots and heritage with pride. The only caveat is that some foreigners may fall prey to using Chinggis Khan and his memory to promote their own value systems and thus, consciously or unconsciously, distort the entire Mongolian process of re-examining their history as they seek a modern, global identity.

The challenge to "invent" a modern Mongolian identity in independent Mongolia is equally felt in other Mongol communities in China and Russia. Identity issues are even more significant for the growing Mongol immigrant Western-based communities living outside the traditional homelands, because they must struggle with what and how to preserve of Mongolian culture while functioning in completely different societies. There is also the question of how should Mongolian peoples respond to other cultures which are expropriating Mongolian iconic symbols as their own national heroes, as China is deliberately doing. Mongolian reaction to the Chi-

---

[69] Byambasuren (2000), 110.

[70] Jehangir S. Pocha, "Mongolia Sees Genghis Khan's Good Side," *International Herald Tribune* (May 10, 2005).

nese attitude of claiming Chinggis Khan as a Chinese hero bears watching.

Other nationalities and culture may soon be claiming Chinggis Khan as their own. In February 2003 an Oxford, England study published in the *American Journal of Human Genetics* on "The Genetic Legacy of the Mongols" estimated that the Mongol leader's blood lineage has more than 17 million direct descendants--one in every 200 people in the world living now, although only one-fifth are present-day Mongolian men![71] A follow-up study by the 2005 Search for Adam television series produced by the National Geo graphic Genographic Project confirmed that the Mongolian leader is the ancestor of about 0.5 percent of the male population of the world today.[72]

Globalization today acts as a catalyst for the urban Mongols to abandon the economic particularities of nomadic culture, and yet this same globalization has brought monied Western cultural preservation organizations to Mongolia to protect and publicize those very same nomad traditions. Integration within the Asian region and world economy will provide both opportunities and challenges in the future for Mongolia, as it struggles to define its post-socialist national identity. This is summed up by economist Byambasuren: "The world that Mongols enters into relation with is entering new development stage and undergoing transition. The world of the 21th century is going to be entirely different from the one of the 20th century. It is going to be the world that lives according [to] globalization and intellectual competition rules. In order to compete and obtain [its] own sustainable position Mongols should have new understanding of themselves and of [the] entire world."[73] It is certain that Mongolian national identity will continue to be closely linked to the image of Chinggis Khan. Less clear is whether or not the Mongols will be proud of the 'universalizing' of their national symbol, Chinggis Khan, or chauvinistically react

---

[71] Nicholas Wade, "A Prolific Genghis Khan, It Seems, Helped People the World," *The New York Times* (February 11, 2003) and Pocha, 2005.

[72] Beth Brophy, "Father of His Country, and Everyone Else," in *Untold Tales of the Great Conquerors* (U.S. News and World Report: 2005) 50-51.

[73] Byambasuren, 2000, 118.

to protect their unique relationship to his image to maintain their national self-identity of *ulus* and *undes.*

BIBLIOGRAPHY

Achenbach, Joel. "The era of his ways," *The Washington Post* (December 31, 1995), F1.

"All Things Considered," National Public Radio, with Robert Siegel, March 25, 2004. In http://www.npr.org/templates/story/story.hp?storyId=1791972.

Ardchilal 7 (Ulaanbaatar: June 1-10, 1990), 4.

Atwood, Christopher. "National Questions and National Answers in the Chinese Revolution, Or, How Do You Say Minzu in Mongolian?" *East Asian Working Paper Series on Language and Politics in Modern China* 5 (Bloomington, 1994), 37-73. In http://www.indiana.edu/easc/resources/working_paper/nofram_5b.htm.

Baabar. *History of Mongolia.* Ulaanbaatar: Monsudar Publishing, 1999.

Batbayar, Tsedendamdyn. *Mongolia's Foreign Policy in the 1990s: New Identity and New Challenges.* Ulaanbaatar: Institute for Strategic Studies, 2002.

________, ed. *Renovation of Mongolia on the Eve of the XXI Century and Future Development Patterns.* Ulaanbaatar: Mongolian Development Research Center, 2000.

Bawden, Charles R. *The Modern History of Mongolia.* New York: Frederick A. Praeger, 1968.

Borchigud, Wurlig. "The Impact of Urban Ethnic Education on Modern Mongolian Ethnicity, 1949-1966." In Harrell, ed. *Cultural Encounters on China's Ethnic Frontiers*, 278-300.

Brooks, James. "Ulan Bator Journal: The Mongolians Are Coming to China! With Heavy Metal! China Frets Over Mongolian Metal Band," *The New York Times* (November 26, 2004). In http://select.nytimes.com/gst/abstract.html?res=F60712FF395A0C758EDDA80994DC404482.

Brophy, Beth. "Father of His Country, and Everyone Else." In *Untold Tales of the Great Conquerors* (U.S. News and World Report, 2005), 50-51.

________. "Rethinking the Legendary Barbarian Genghis Khan." In *Untold Tales of the Great Conquerors* (U.S. News and World Report, 2005), 46-51.

Brown, Melissa J., ed. *Negotiating Ethnicities in China and Taiwan.* Berkeley: Institute of East Asian Studies, 1996.

Bulag, Uradyn E. "The Chinese Cult of Chinggis Khan: Genealogical Nationalism and Problems of National and Cultural Integrity." Unpublished paper. Victoria, B.C., October 3-5, 2003. In http://www.smhric.org/E_Bulag_2.pdf

________. *The Mongols at China's Edge: History and the Politics of National Unity.* Lanham: Rowman & Littlefield, 2002.

Byambasuren, D. "National Factors Affecting Development Strategy of Mongolia." In Batbayar, ed. *Renovation of Mongolia on the Eve of the XXI Century and Future Development Patterns*, 106-121.

Dashpurev, D., and S.K. Soni. *Reign of Terror in Mongolia 1920-1990.* New Delhi: South Asian Publishers, 1992.

Gardi, Borjigin. "In Inner Mongolia, Tribe Resists Bid to Turn Shrine into a Theme Park," Radio Free Asia (February 17, 2005). In www.smhric.org/news-75.htm.

"Genghis Khan's New Fan Club," *The London Times* (June 1,1980).

Harrell, Stevan, ed. *Cultural Encounters on China's Ethnic Frontiers.* Seattle and London: University of Washington Press, 1995.

History of the Mongolian People's Republic. Moscow: Nauka Publishing House, 1973.

"In Search of Chinggis Khaan," *Mongolia Today Online Magazine* 2 (2000), in www.mongoliatoday.com/issue/2/tomb_mistery.html.

Kaplonski, Christopher. "Creating National Identity in Socialist Mongolia," *Central Asian Survey* 17 (1998), 35-49.

Khan, Almaz. "Chinggis Khan: From Imperial Ancestor to Ethnic Hero." In Harrell, ed. *Cultural Encounters on China's Ethnic Frontiers*, 248-277.

________. "Who Are the Mongols? State, Ethnicity, and the Politics of Representation in the PRC." In Brown, ed. *Negotiating Ethnicities in China and Taiwan*, 125-159.

Kristof, Nicholas. "Where Genghis Khan Is In," *The New York*

Times Magazine (May 27, 1990), Section 6, 21-23. In http://select.nytimes.com/gst/abstract.html?res=F30616F83C540C748EDDAC0894D8494D81.

Manduhai, Buyandelgeriyn. "The Spirit of My Homeland is Recalling Me: Nationalism, Landscape, and Ritual Among the Buriats of Mongolia." Abstract. Boston: Central Eurasian Studies Society 4th Annual Conference (October 2003).

Munkh-Erdene, Lkhamsuren. "Inquiry to Mongolian Nationalism Through Terms and Concepts, from Late Nineteenth Century to Mid-1920s". Unpublished paper. Sapporo, 2004.

Murphy, David. "No Room for Nomads," *Far Eastern Economic Review* (May 31, 2001), 122-143.

Nyamtseren, L. "Main Developmental Pattern of Mongolia in the Edge of the 21 Century." In Batbayar, ed. *Renovation of Mongolia on the Eve of the XXI Century and Future Development Patterns*, 122-143.

Osborn, Andrew. "The Cult of Genghis Khan," *Independent News* (London: May 11, 2005). In http://news.independent.co.uk/world/asia/article220947.ece.

Pegg, Carole. *Mongolian Music, Dance, and Oral Narrative.* Seattle and London: University of Washington Press, 2001.

Pocha, Jehangir S. "Mongolia Sees Genghis Khan's Good Side," *International Herald Tribune* (May 10, 2005). In http://www.iht.com/articles/2005/05/09/news/mongol.php.

"The Political Report of the First Congress of the Mongolian Social-Democratic Party" (March 31, 1990), 14.

Quammen, David. "In the Kingdom of Eternal Blue Heaven," *National Geographic Adventure* (January 2006), 88-95, 100-103.

Sabloff, Paula, ed. *Modern Mongolia: Reclaiming Genghis Khan.* Philadelphia: University of Pennsylvania Museum of Archaeology and Anthropology, 2001.

Sandag, Shagdaryn, and Harry H. Kendall. *Poisoned Arrows: The Stalin-Choibalsan Mongolian Massacres, 1921-1941*. Boulder: Westview Press, 2000.

Soni, Sharad K. *Mongolia-Russia Relations: Kiakhta to Vladivostok.* Delhi: Shipra Publications, 2002.

Wade, Nicholas. "A Prolific Genghis Khan, It Seems, Helped People the World," *The New York Times* (February 11, 2003). In http://query.nytimes.com/gst/fullpage.html?sec=health&res =9C02EFD.

Weatherford, Jack. *Genghis Khan and the Making of the Modern World.* New York: Crown Press, 2004.

www.economicexpert.com/a/buryat.htm.

www.kalmykiaembassy.ru/html/ehistory/html.

Globalization in Mongolia: Cultural Evidence from the *UB Post*

Mei-hua Lan

As a communist country from 1924 to 1990, Mongolia was subjected to overwhelming Soviet influence in all areas, including journalism where Mongolia's equivalent to *Pravda* was a newspaper called *Ünen*. However, with the coming of democratization in 1990, Mongolia's freedom of the press has been improved,[1] and a large number of newspapers and journals, including English-language newspapers, have appeared on the market. At the same time, the press and all other facets of Mongolian society have been severely impacted by the forces of globalization.

The purpose of my paper is to examine the impact of globalization in Mongolia by analyzing the information provided by the *UB Post* in a period of about four months, from No. 454 of February 3 to No. 472 of June 9, 2005. Although the *UB Post* is only a weekly newspaper, it does provide the most important news of an entire week to its readers.[2] Each issue has eight pages and

---

[1] According to the statistics of Freedom House, Mongolia was a country of no press freedom in the Soviet era, became a country of partly press freedom since 1990, and was even ranked as a country of press freedom in the years of 1992 and 1999-2001. See various publications of the press freedom survey of Freedom House, http://www.freedomhouse.org/research/pressurvey.htm (accessed 23 June 2005).

[2] The readership of the *UB Post* is primarily foreigners in Ulaanbaatar, but Mongols interested in learning English such as students of English departments are also its possible readers. The domestic news of the *UB Post* is covered by its reporters or translated from major Mongolian newspapers. Foreign news is usually pieces from major news agencies of the West, China, Russia, or other Asian countries. They are important news pieces that also appear in other major

cost 500 tugrig (about 45 cents) in early 2005. The results will tell us more about the present situation of Mongolia in the era of globalization.

THE UB POST

MONGOLIA'S INDEPENDENT WEEKLY NEWS

TODAY

MOBICOM DIRECTOR AND MP CLASH OVER PRICING

Next week's UB Post will be on sale on Tuesday February 8, instead of the usual Thursday publication. This is due to the Tsagaan Sar holiday

Mongol News chief awarded

Demonstration against corruption to block road

Cabinet donates tsunami aid from state reserve

Driver found dead in trunk

LEARNING FOREIGN LANGUAGES

Learning foreign languages is now very popular in Mongolia. It has been my experience that Mongols are good at learning foreign languages. They are not afraid of saying a wrong sentence or using a wrong expression. I am personally acquainted with several scholars who did not learn their English in any formal education but through self-study at home and learning from other English speakers at their job sites, and it is not uncommon to find Mongols who can speak more than one language.

This linguistic facility seems to be deeply rooted in history. In the thirteenth century, during the time of the Mongolian world empire, many Mongols were known to be conversant in the various languages, such as Chinese, Tibetan, Persian, and the many Turkic languages, spoken in history's largest contiguous empire.

---

newspapers in Mongolia. Although part of the stories or articles appearing in the *UB Post* are chosen for its particular readership and may be not of major concern of ordinary Mongols, they also tell us some aspects of the life in Mongolia and the attitude of the newspaper toward its foreign readers.

When Tibetan Buddhism became a popular religious belief among the Mongols in the sixteenth century, education in Mongolia came under the control of the Buddhist monasteries, and Tibetan became the language of instruction as well as the canonical and liturgical language.

Later, when the Mongols came under Manchu rule, Chinese merchants eventually became economically dominant, and as a consequence Chinese became an important and useful language for the Mongols to learn. Ma Hetian, a Chinese agent who traveled in Mongolia in 1926-27, observed that many Mongol women who served as temporary wives of Chinese merchants learned Chinese, wore semi-Chinese clothes, even played Chinese musical instruments, sang Chinese songs, and arranged their dwellings entirely in a Chinese fashion.[3] Mongolian women learned Chinese to serve their temporary husbands, and men learned Chinese for economic, political, and cultural use. During the Soviet era, Mongols began to learn Russian in their elementary schools, and many of them continued their higher education in Russia. It is no surprise, therefore, that during the seven decades of Russian dominance the most spoken foreign language in Mongolia was Russian.

Since the collapse of the Soviet Union and the democratic reform in Mongolia, the official policy of Russian as the second language was abandoned, and English is now taught at the elementary school level. English is also popular outside the school. When you enter a bookstore in Ulaanbaatar, you can easily find English textbooks, dictionaries, and other learning materials. The replacement of Russian by English as the main foreign language clearly indicates Mongolia's turning from Russia to the United States and its opening to the capitalist world.

The reason for this shift to English is not difficult to find. A language is not only a system for communication or a culture carrier, but also a symbol of power. Knowledge of English has become a necessity mainly because the United States is perceived as the most powerful country in the world. In order to survive or find an adequate position in the new capitalistic and global era,

---

[3] Ma Ho-t'ien, *Chinese agent in Mongolia: A report on the birth of the Mongolian People's Republic*, tr. John De Francis (Baltimore: The Johns Hopkins Press, 1949), 128.

Mongols are trying hard to learn foreign languages, and above all, English. To what extent some Mongols are willing to go to learn English and the culture it represents is reflected in this recent incident. It is reported that in 2005 two Mongolian university students went to London to participate in an international public speaking competition hosted by the English Speaking Union. Although neither student was selected to attend the final, they said that their main aim was not to win first prize, but to "participate and get in contact with people around the world," and the trip to the United Kingdom "opened their eyes to a very different lifestyle."[4]

Every issue of the *UB Post* during the period under consideration had a weekly ad for language teachers: "Native speaking English, German, Japanese language teachers wanted," with English always listed first. There was also a separate ad for recruiting only English teachers.[5] Ads of two international schools appeared regularly in the newspaper. One was the International School of Ulaanbaatar,[6] and the other the Ulaanbaatar Elite International School.[7] Although their students are from several different countries, English dominates these schools' curricula.[8] The paper also published news about Mongolian students studying in the United States[9] and Canada.[10]

Another Western language that is currently rising in popularity mostly among young Mongols is German. This popularity is partly due to historical circumstances. During the Soviet era, many Mon-

---

[4] "English language competition fosters international connections," *The UB Post*, 9 June 2005, 2.

[5] "Classifieds," "Teacher wanted," *The UB Post*, 9 June 2005, 3.

[6] These ads appear in *The UB Post* on February 17 (p. 4), May 5 (p. 3), May 12 (p. 5), May 19 (p. 5), June 1 (p. 3), and June 8 (p. 5) of 2005.

[7] These ads appear in *The UB Post* on April 28 (p. 3), May 5 (p. 5), May 12 (p. 5), May 19 (p. 5), May 26 (p. 3), June 1 (p. 6), and June 8 (p. 3) of 2005.

[8] According to the web site of International School of Ulaanbaatar, "ISU offers Mongolia's only internationally recognized curriculum in English. All classes are taught in English." See "Curriculum," International School of Ulaanbaatar, http://www.isumongolia.org/index.php?option=content&task=blogcategory&id=12&Itemid=38 (accessed 1 December 2005).

[9] "Trip to Illinois concretes education," *The UB Post*, 31 March 2005, 5.

[10] "Learning as an international experience: Canadian project crosses borders in education," *The UB Post*, 1 June 2005, 5.

gols worked and studied in the German Democratic Republic, now the eastern part of a reunited Germany. Another, perhaps even more important reason for German being studied by a growing number of Mongols is Germany's economic power. The Mongolian government considers Germany its leading European partner. So far, about thirty German firms have invested in Mongolia. These include several joint enterprises such as the beer company Khan Bräu, the Mercedes-Benz representative VITSAMO, and Lufthansa Technik's cooperation with the Mongolian national airline MIAT.[11] Moreover, since the early 1990s some German-speaking Mongols have gone to Germany in hopes of finding a better life.

The sharp rise since the early 1990s in the use of English, German and other Western languages has resulted in what some Mongols consider a flood of advertising and other signs all over Ulaanbaatar using the Latin alphabet. Opponents of this trend have sought to reverse it by promoting a cause initiated mostly by academics to make the Mongolian script the country's official script.[12] On March 1, 2005, the newspaper *Khumuun Bichig*, which is printed in traditional Mongolian script, made an appeal against the use of the Latin alphabet for business names and signs. The appeal is intended to be a part of the "Traditional Mongol Script Day" on May 1.[13]

Unlike English and other Western languages, Japanese and Korean have witnessed a sharp rise in popularity among Mongols only partly because of economic and political reasons but mostly for their linguistic and cultural similarities. The structure of Mongolian, Japanese, and Korean are so close that people who speak any one of the three languages can easily learn the other two. I recall that in 1993 a Korean student studying in Ulaanbaatar told me that it was almost too easy for him to learn Mongolian, espe-

---

11 "Mongolia," Federal Foreign Office of Germany, http://www.auswaertiges-amt.de/www/en/laenderinfos/laender/laender_ausgabe_html?type_id=14&land_id=115 (accessed 27 June 2005).

12 "About Mongolia," Embassy of Mongolia, Washington D.C., http://www.mongolianembassy.us/eng_about_mongolia/land_and_people.php (accessed 26 June 2005).

13 "Appeal against Latin alphabet," *The UB Post*, 3 March 2005, 1.

cially conversation. All he needed to do was to substitute the Korean with Mongolian words. In the same year, a Japanese restaurant owner told me that reading Mongolian was not very difficult for him, but that correct pronunciation demanded a lot of effort. Books and other materials for learning Japanese and Korean languages are for sale in most bookstores. There are also radio and television programs teaching the two "related" languages.

Most Mongols who learn Japanese and Korean wish to study in or find a job related to the two countries.[14] To many Mongols,

[14] There are approximately 20,000 Mongols in South Korea. Many of them work there illegally. According to the *UB Post*, Korean immigration officials said on February 5 that they deported seven Mongols for illegal stay and were seeking seven more from the same group. "Twelve Mongols Deported from South Korea," *The UB Post*, 8 February, 2005, 5. Since there is a Mongolian community in South Korea, Mongolian artists also go to Korea to perform for their countrymen. For instance, Nomin Talst, a famous Mongolian pop music group, had its first overseas concert in Seoul for the Mongolian audience during the past Tsagaan Sar holidays. Paul Bacon, "Nomin Talst Play Seoul Music," *The*

Japan and South Korea are role models because they are Asian and therefore culturally closer than Europe and America. This perception has helped popularize certain Japanese and Korean products and styles. Readers can find in the *UB Post* ads of a dental clinic that emphasizes its "Japanese management,"[15] and an ad inviting people to buy private houses built "in Korean style"[16] (see the illustration on the preceding page).

As mentioned by Migeddorj Batchimeg, a senior researcher at the Institute for Strategic Studies of Mongolia, while Russia still enjoys certain political and economic influence in Mongolia, it is now China which is emerging as the main political and economic partner of Mongolia.[17] Therefore, a growing number of Mongols have come to perceive the learning of Chinese as an important and necessary goal. So far, China's booming market is probably the main reason for the Mongols to learn Chinese. Anyone who masters Chinese can easily find a decent job in a Mongolian company, as evidenced by some of my Mongolian friends. However, it has proven much more difficult to work for a Chinese company. Almost every Chinese group visiting Mongolia, no matter whether it is official or private, brings along a Mongol from Inner Mongolia as its own interpreter, probably because the members of these groups trust their "own" Mongols more.

INTERNATIONAL CUISINE

In the entertainment section on the back page of the *UB Post*, there are usually recipes or restaurant reviews. Besides, the ads of

---

UB Post, 17 February, 2005, 6. Because there is an increase in the number of Korean tourists who visit Mongolia, Korean Airlines decided to increase its flights from Seoul to Ulaanbaatar starting June 1, 2005. "Increase in Korean Air Flights," *The UB Post*, 7 April, 2005, 1.

[15] The same ad of Hope Dental Clinic appeared in every issue of *The UB Post* from February 8 to April 21, 2005. It always appeared on page 3.

[16] "Komodo village," *The UB Post*, 21 April 2005, 7.

[17] Migeddorj Batchimeg, "Future challenges for the PRC and Mongolia: A Mongolian perspective," The Jamestown Foundation, http://jamestown.org/publications_details.php?volume_id=408&issue_id=3322&article_id=2369704 (accessed 27 June 2005).

some restaurants also appear often in the newspaper. The readers can taste an international flavor via these short essays and ads. During the period of my investigation, recipes appeared of foods from Russia,[18] Korea,[19] Italy,[20] China,[21] and Middle East.[22] Ads of the Hazara Indian Restaurant (see illustration on next page), Taj Mahal Indian Restaurant, Los Bandidos Indian and Mexican Restaurant, and the Detroit American Bar (see illustration on next page) were regular features in the newspaper, while an ad of Le Bistrot [sic] Français appeared once.[23] Although only a relatively few Mongols are able to afford eating out at such exotic restaurants, many others may enjoy cooking some foreign dishes at home with the help of the recipes in the *UB Post*. What seems beyond dispute is that the culinary scene in Ulaanbaatar has acquired a more cosmopolitan flavor.

During my trips to Ulaanbaatar in the last decade, I could clearly notice a growing interest in foreign cuisine. There are more choices than the options mentioned above. During the Soviet era, in addition to traditional Mongolian food, only Russian and certain European foods were available, but since the early 1990s cuisines from many other countries have appeared as a symbol of Mongolia's new openness. For example, fried chicken and hamburgers are presented as Mongolia's opening to the United States: an ad for the Detroit American Bar proudly announced that "The Motor City Comes to Ulaanbaatar."[24] This establishment is seen not just as a bar, but as an American icon transplanted onto Mongolian soil. Such advertisements are, of course, motivated by the

---

[18] Iryna Po[e]psel, "A Hunger for Russian Food," *The UB Post*, 3 February 2005, 7; Iryna Poepsel, "No. 5: Kotletas," *The UB Post*, 24 February 2005, 8.

[19] Iryna Poepsel, "Korean Gem Hidden in Deepest Bayanzurkh," *The UB Post*, 17 February 2005, 8; James Brown Park, "Seoul Food," *The UB Post*, 9 June 2005, 8.

[20] Iryna Poepsel, "Italian Cuisine in Ulaanbaatar," *The UB Post*, 10 March 2005, 7; Todd Smith, "No. 9: Aglio e Olio," *The UB Post*, 21 April 2005, 7.

[21] Moe Kholl, "Help, I'm Locked Inside a Chinese Cookie Factory," *The UB Post*, 28 April 2005, 7; Howie Ba, "The Chinese Are Coming, the Chinese Are Coming," *The UB Post*, 26 May 2005, 8.

[22] Isabela Irra, "A Piece of the Middle East," *The UB Post*, 21 April 2005, 7.

[23] *The UB Post*, 3 March 2005, 3.

[24] *The UB Post*, 26 May 2005, 4.

ultimate aim in the new capitalistic market which is to attract customers and thus bring in more money.

After official diplomatic relations were established between Mongolia and South Korea in March 1990, the ties of friendship and cooperation between the two countries have steadily developed in various fields, including diplomacy, economics, and culture. Currently thousands of Mongols work legally or illegally in South Korea to send funds to relatives back home. Due to good quality and reasonable prices, Korean products can be easily found on the Mongolian market and Korean soap operas are warmly received by Mongolian audiences. When it comes to food, kimchi, a national Korean spicy vegetable pickled and seasoned with garlic, red pepper, and ginger, now appears on the dining table in many Mongolian households even though traditional Mongolian dishes have been known to be rarely spicy. A Mongolian scholar told me that his family began to enjoy kimchi after his sojourn in Seoul as a visiting scholar. For him kimchi is not only a dish but also something symbolizing his family's tie with Korea.

To me, the most significant change in foreign cuisine is the rapid increase in the number of Chinese restaurants in Ulaanbaatar. When I stayed there for six months in 1993, I could find only a couple of

Chinese restaurants in the city. However, according to a restaurant review in the *UB Post*, the author learned from a recent publication of the Department of Non-Mongolian Foods in the Ministry of Edible and Non-Edible Comestibles that there are now 234 Chinese restaurants in Ulaanbaatar.[25] The author of another restaurant review easily listed eleven Chinese restaurants in Ulaanbaatar.[26] This marks the reversal of a recent historical trend. Prior to the split between China and the Soviet Union in the mid-1960s, relations between Mongolia and China were friendly and cooperative. There were many Chinese living in Mongolia, Chinese food was popular, and many Chinese restaurants existed in Mongolia. During the split, however, Mongolia had no choice but to stand on the side of the Soviet Union, and its relations with China plummeted. They got so bad that in 1983, Mongolia began to systematically expel some of the 7,000 ethnic Chinese in Mongolia to China. Many of them had lived in Mongolia since the 1950s, when they were sent there to assist in construction projects.[27] Another victim of that policy were Chinese restaurants in Mongolia whose numbers greatly decreased.

How authentic the various foreign cuisines in Mongolia are is not important in this discussion. Restaurant owners and managers are modifying the taste of their dishes to attract more Mongolian customers. The important thing is that the large variety of foreign cuisines, especially those from countries currently popular in Mongolia, testifies to the influence of globalization and Mongolia's eagerness to open its doors to the world.

THE ARRIVAL OF CHRISTIANITY

The Mongols were known for their religious tolerance in the thirteenth century. Their practice of religious tolerance was not

---

[25] Moe Kholl, "Help, I'm Locked Inside a Chinese Cookie Factory." The number may include all restaurants or eating places where so-called Chinese food is provided. The author of the article complains that one can find bad Chinese food just about anywhere in Ulaanbaatar.

[26] Howie Ba, "The Chinese Are Coming, the Chinese Are Coming."

[27] "Background Note: Mongolia," U.S. Department of State, http://www.state.gov/r/pa/ei/bgn/2779.htm (accessed 26 June 2005).

only a demonstration of self-confidence on the part of leaders like Chinggis Khan, but also a positive factor that helped them to create the Mongol world empire. Besides shamanism and Buddhism, Islam and Christianity were also practiced among the people within the Mongol empire.

With the return of Buddhism to Mongolia at the end of the sixteenth century, many Mongols became devoted Buddhists. Being a lama became commonplace and the number of Buddhist monasteries and temples increased significantly. Buddhism became an inseparable part of the Mongolian tradition. When the Manchus rose to power in the seventeenth century, they tried to put the religion of the Mongols under their control, but they did not challenge their religious belief and actually became strong promoters of Buddhism. As for the Mongols, they continued to practice religious tolerance and did not try to convert believers of other religions to Buddhism.

While Mongolia came under the sway of the Soviet Union in the 1920s, Russian atheism and materialism started to have a profound effect in the entire country. Religious practice gradually became a taboo which resulted in a decline in the people's commitment to Buddhism, but the religion never entirely vanished from Mongolia. With the coming of democratization in the 1990s, Mongolian traditional culture began to regain its importance, and the revitalization of Buddhism and shamanism is part of this process. The Mongolian government is making use of some traditional metaphors to emphasize Mongolia's genuine independence, and common people embrace their cultural heritage to help themselves cope with the difficulties that followed the enormous changes in the early 1990s.

One of the consequences of democratization and globalization has been the arrival of Christianity in Mongolia. Actually, one could speak of a return because back in the thirteenth century Nestorian Christianity appeared to have had a presence in some parts of Mongolia, but their influence vanished a long time ago. The present influx of Christianity started, according to information supplied by Serving in Mission, an international Christian mission agency, with Christian radio programs, but the churches that have subsequently been established are thoroughly Mongolian, and an estimated 20,000 believers now live in Mongolia.[28] Some Mongols have become Christians because they accept the teachings of that religion while others do so because they want to build a connection to the outside world, especially to the West.

In the *UB Post*, a joint ad of the International English Speaking Christian Fellowship and the Mongolian Bible Teaching Seminar appear almost every week. Christ Fellowship of Mongolia once published an ad for an "English praise and worship evening" in the newspaper.[29] Another ad was an invitation for people to participate in a "one-hour non-stop praise and worship."[30] I know some Filipino and Korean missionaries who serve devotedly in Ulaanbaatar while keeping a low profile. The Mongolian government was very suspicious of foreign missionaries in the early 1990s, so the latter had to disguise their true identity and held meetings secretly in private homes. Now conditions for missionaries has considerably improved but is still not without problems.

Besides news about Bible teaching, praise, and worship, other Christian activities, the *UB Post* also included an item about President N. Bagabandi sending a telegram to the Vatican to convey his condolences over the death of Pope John Paul II,[31] and another item featured his congratulatory message to the newly-elected Pope Benedict XVI and Mongolian Catholics rejoicing for Pope Benedict XVI.[32] In another ad in the *UB Post*, I noticed that Korean missionaries established an elementary school to educate Korean children in Ulaanbaatar that offered both a Korean and an English curriculum.[33]

Under the influence of democratization and globalization, Christianity returned to Mongolia. If the country continues its democratization efforts, Christianity as well as other religions will

---

28 "Mongolia," Serving in Mission, http://www.sim.co.uk/where/mongolia.htm (accessed 27 June 2005).

29 *The UB Post*, 19 May 2005, 2.

30 *The UB Post*, 9 June 2005, 4.

31 "President Sends Telegram to the Vatican," *The UB Post*, 7 April 2005, 1.

32 "Mongolian Catholics Rejoice for Pope Benedict XVI," *The UB Post*, 28 April 2005, 1.

33 "Ulaanbaatar MK School," *The UB Post*, 26 May 2005, 5.

continue to gain adherents in Mongolia, but Buddhism and shamanism are like to remain more influential.

PROSTITUTION AND TRAFFICKING OF WOMEN

An article in the March 24 issue, entitled "The Dark Side of Casino Lights" described how Mongolian girls were trafficked to Macao by other Mongolian women to become prostitutes. The article was based on an interview of a 21-year-old woman with the pseudonym Bolor that was originally printed in the newspaper *Mongoliin Medee* on March 18.

According to the interview, Bolor was betrayed by her girl friend and taken to Macao instead of Singapore where she had wanted to study English. She ended up working as a prostitute in a sauna which employed forty women, fully half of them being Mongols. The women worked from eight in the evening until eight in the morning. On average, each woman served at least five customers per night, and sometimes up to fifteen on busy nights. All women signed six-month contracts with the sauna manager who confiscated their passports so they could not escape. After they had worked for six months, each woman was allowed to return home for a few days, but they are obliged to enlist another woman from their homeland. They are offered a large commission for successfully recruiting another woman to the sauna.

Bolor said, "There are a lot of Mongolian women working as prostitutes in Macao, in karaoke venues, bars, swimming pools, saunas, and other places of entertainment." Most of the women knew in advance they would work as prostitutes, but a few were cheated and trafficked to Macao. She hopes that the Mongolian government will take measures against prostitution and to protect girls who live on the street. She said that street girls as young as fourteen and fifteen years of age are often trafficked to Macao, Singapore and Malaysia.[34]

Due to the economic hardships that followed the political and economic changes in the early 1990s and more foreigners coming

---

[34] "The Dark Side of Casino Lights," *The UB Post*, 24 March 2005, 4.

to Mongolia from richer capitalist countries, prostitution as a phenomenon of a market economy began to appear in Mongolia. There were no laws prohibiting sexual harassment until September 2002,[35] but even after banning prostitution in that year, the practice has spread among girls and women and there are private individuals and groups who make money from acting as their agents. As early as in 1997, there were one thousand instances of prostitution registered with the police in Ulaanbaatar alone.[36] In 2002, the official registration figures came down to sixty-one, but a study conducted by the Mongolian National University in 2001 found that 200-250 girls in Ulaanbaatar were involved in prostitution. Most of them were living away from home without supervision and had previously suffered sexual abuse.[37]

The increase in child labor and the number of street children owing to poverty and poverty-driven domestic abuse also provided a source for commercial sex. According to a pilot survey conducted in 1998 by the Women's Information and Research Center and Save the Children Fund, there were approximately 400 girls engaged in sex work in Ulaanbaatar. Depending on where they worked, the girls were paid from two to six dollars per hour and from six to fifteen dollars per night.[38]

Among the eighteen interviewees, 66.7% of the girls answered that they became sex workers to earn money and 38.9% because it was part of the street life. Most of the girls live on the street and some of their families also live on the street. The factors and reasons for the girls to become sex workers were inadequate home

---

[35] "Mongolia," Country Reports on Human Rights Practices – 2002, U.S. Department of State, http://www.state.gov/g/drl/rls/hrrpt/2002/18255.htm (accessed 4 July 2005).

[36] National Human Rights Commission of Mongolia and Centre for Human Rights and Development, "The crime of trafficking of women and children in Mongolia: The current situation," (Ulaanbaatar: November 2002), 9, http://www.owc.org.mn/chrd/publication/Trafficking%20Report%202002-eng.doc (accessed 4 July 2005).

[37] "Juvenile Justice in Mongolia," 13, UNICEF – Mongolia, http://mirror.undp.org/mongolia/publications/JJ_Eng.pdf (accessed 6 July 2005).

[38] "Girls as Sex Workers: Situation and Trends in Mongolia," Gender Center for Sustainable Development, http://www.wirc.mn/research/page4.htm (accessed 3 July 2005).

environment, poverty, conflict in the family, and a lack of appropriate relationships between parents and children. For the girls themselves, there were two reasons for being engaged in sex work. They felt the need to earn money in order to support their low-income or unemployed families, and as street girls they regarded prostitution as their only viable option. Another important reason given by these interviewees was their very low self-esteem. Having suffered poverty, hunger, and ultimately being looked down upon by others, especially by other young people, these women saw in prostitution their way to better clothing, food, and other opportunities.[39]

The country report on human rights of the U.S. Department of State also indicates that some female and teenage citizens of Mongolia worked in the sex trade in Asia and Eastern Europe, and an unknown number of them may have been trafficked. In 2003, the national police documented 148 cases of underage prostitution. In that same year, police investigated seven cases involving nineteen suspects accused of trafficking sixty women to Hong Kong, Macao, and South Korea. During the year, non-governmental organizations reported that seven women were trafficked to Poland from the country. Authorities detained and subsequently denied entry to two foreign nationals (one British and one South Korean) for alleged trafficking of women.[40] The need of foreigners for commercial sex will be probably on the increase if Mongolia continues to carry on economic reforms towards a market economy.

According to the joint report of the National Human Rights Commission of Mongolia and the Center for Human Rights and Development, there are circumstances within Mongolian society today that are suited to the trafficking of humans. These include a direct relationship between negative social phenomena that have arisen as a result of Mongolia's transition to capitalism. Some of these phenomena are increased poverty, unemployment, and prostitution among women as well as drug use among youth, illegal emigration of citizens abroad, illegal labor of Mongolian citizens

---

[39] "Girls as Sex Workers: Situation and Trends in Mongolia."

[40] "Mongolia," Country Reports on Human Rights Practices 2004, U. S. Department of State. In http://www.state.gov/g/drl/rls/hrrpt/2004/41652.htm (accessed 3 July 2005).

in foreign countries (including the manufacturing of false visas and passports), and an increased interest among girls and women to marry foreigners. All of these factors contribute to an environment in which the crime of trafficking can occur. In addition, a lack of knowledge about life abroad and naive attitudes in trusting different kinds of mediators are some of the factors that have led to trafficking.[41]

Prostitutes face a particularly high risk of becoming the object of trafficking, according to a research conducted by the Center for Human Rights and Development (CHRD) in 2003. The center interviewed 124 prostitutes in Ulaanbaatar, Darhan, Choibalsan, Zamyn-Uud and the Chinese town of Erlian, as well as seventeen women and girls working in nightclubs and bars in Ulaanbaatar. Almost a quarter of them were ready to accept proposals to go overseas for well-paid work if their expenses were covered. The survey concluded that sales of people take place not only overseas, but also in Mongolia. Bringing girls and young women from rural regions to big cities and towns for prostitution has become a widespread business. 28.2% of the prostitutes responded that they had been sold forcibly, proving that they are under the patronage of pimps.[42]

In all of the trafficking cases that the CHRD documented, the women were recruited and transported abroad for the purpose of coerced prostitution, after being deceived about the nature and/or conditions of the "employment" awaiting them. Most women were required to sign contracts, but they were not told about the debts they would "owe" nor were they aware of the dangers they were about to face. The recruiters were mostly Mongols, working in cooperation with agents abroad, and the recruits tended to be young, single women who are unemployed, students, and/or already engaged in prostitution. Traffickers lured their victims with promises of high paying jobs, training, education, and/or assistance in marrying foreigners.

---

[41] "The crime of trafficking of women and children in Mongolia: The current situation," 7.

[42] "People Trafficking on the Rise," *The Mongol Messenger*, http://www.mongolmessenger.mn/issue/040207.php (accessed 6 July 2005).

According to the research findings, there are many suspicious recruitment advertisements for women in the Mongolian press including ads for virgins and specifications about women's physical appearance. Although recruiters for overseas employment are required to obtain a licence from the Ministry of Social Welfare, in reality there is no mechanism for monitoring or enforcing this regulation. Ulaanbaatar and other major urban centers such as Darkhan and Erdenet are the main recruitment centers for traffickers, and Macao is the most common destination, although Mongol women are also trafficked to China, other parts of Asia, and even to Europe.[43] It is obvious that girls and women make up the majority of humans trafficked abroad, and many of them are engaged in prostitution.

Prostitution is new in post-communist Mongolia, but it is certainly not new in Mongolia. Ma Ho-t'ien mentions in his diary that prostitutes in Urga (today's Ulaanbaatar) were said to total two or three thousand. They included quite a few Russians and Japan-ese as well as Mongols. Most of the Russians who engaged in prostitution were Buriats, and more than a hundred Japanese women had embraced that profession.[44] In the 1920s, because the power of Chinese merchants was still overwhelming in Mongolia, many clients of the prostitutes were Chinese merchants. At pre-sent, the clients are not limited to Chinese. They include other foreigners as well as Mongols, but Japanese women are no longer working as sex workers in Mongolia.

MONGOLIAN SUMO WRESTLERS IN JAPAN

The last page of each issue of the *UB Post* features the sports section which is frequently dominated by news concerning Mongolian sumo wrestlers and tournaments. The issue of February 3 reported the outstanding record of Mongolian sumo players in Tokyo. The news read, "All-in-all six men from the steppe posted

---

[43] Centre for Human Rights and Development, "Combating human trafficking in Mongolia: issues and opportunities," Ulaanbaatar 2003-2004, http://www.asiafoundation.org/pdf/Mongolia-trafficking.pdf (accessed 6 July 2005).
[44] Ma Ho-t'ien, *Chinese agent in Mongolia*, 128-129.

winning records in Tokyo." It continued, "These contemporary Mongols are succeeding where their thirteenth century compatriots failed -- in completing a successful invasion of Japan. Over seven hundred years ago two violent storms helped repel Mongolian armies from the shores of Kyushu. From there the legend of kamikaze was born. This time, however, there appears to be no divine wind powerful enough to stop the modern Mongolian hordes." The news also mentioned the anxiety of the Japanese by quoting a Japanese news headline saying, "Foreigners head for total domination of sumo."[45] Foreign sumo wrestlers in Japan come not only from Mongolia, but also from Bulgaria, Georgia, Russia, Estonia, the Czech Republic, Kazakhstan, Hungary, South Korea, China, Brazil, and Tonga. However, more than thirty Mongolian wrestlers are currently participating in sumo tournaments and they constitute more than half of the foreign sumo wrestlers in Japan.[46] Under the impact of market economy and globalization, sumo wrestling is not only a traditional sport for the Japanese, but also a game of international stature.

Among the three manly sports of the Mongols, wrestling is the most popular. The top wrestlers are national heroes. After Mongolia began its democratic reforms and turned toward a market economy, many Mongols opened their eyes to foreign countries to find their opportunities. For Mongolian wrestlers, Japanese sumo wrestling is a perfect stage for them to try out. Mongolian sumo wrestlers soon earned their place in Japan. Their pictures appear in Mongolia's newspapers, magazines, posters, calendars, and even political campaign material. Famous sumo wrestlers such as Asashoryu D. Dagvadorj, Kyokushuzan D. Batbayar, and Kyokutenho N. Tsevegnyam became national heroes among the Mongols due to their great achievements and victories in professional sumo wrestling. They were even awarded with medals and honored as "Image Ambassador of Mongolia" by the Mongolian National Chamber of Commerce and Industry because of their "contributions to promulgating and glorifying Mongolia abroad, extending

---

45 "Gambare Nippon! Native Sumo Subjugated by Foreign Conquerors," *The UB Post*, 3 February 2005, 8.

46 "All sumo foreign rikishi," http://moti.sumogames.com/tForeigners.htm (accessed 11 July 2005).

foreign relations, and promoting business and foreign investments."[47]

D. Batbayar is one of the three pioneer Mongolian wrestlers who went to participate in sumo wrestling back in 1992.[48] His ring name is Kyokushuzan and highest rank is komusubi, the fourth highest rank in sumo.[49] He is known as a "supermarket of tricks" among sumo fans. It is said that he has brought innovation and dynamics to the traditional sumo wrestling by using Mongolian wrestling techniques and even tricks long forgotten by Japanese sumo wrestlers. Most Japanese agree that sumo wrestling became different after Batbayar entered the arena. His successful debut in sumo had encouraged many young Mongols to try out this new field and caused a surge in interest in sumo wrestling among the Mongols.[50] In sumo, sheer size is no substitute for technique. Mongolian sumo wrestlers are witness of this point. A Japanese web proclaims that "the powerfully built Mongolian wrestlers dazzle the eye with their crisply executed throwing techniques and are creating a new trend that favors technique over size."[51] This is the contribution of Mongolian wrestlers to sumo.

Asashoryu Akinori, born as Dolgorsuren Dagvadorj in Ulaanbaatar, went to Japan in 1997 and made his professional debut in January 1999. When he gained the status of ozeki, the second highest rank in sumo, in July 2002, he was not only the first Mongolian and fourth foreign wrestler ever to reach this rank, but also the fastest to do so since 1958.[52] Asashoryu also became the first

---

47 "Database: Inspiring Mongolia," Mongolian National Chamber of Commerce and Industry, http://www.mongolchamber.mn/en/modules.php? name =News&file=article&sid=110 (accessed 11 July 2005).

48 "A Sumo Pioneer," *Kansai Time Out*, no. 333, November 2004, http://www.kto.co.jp/2004nov/article4.html (accessed 12 July 2005).

49 "Kyokushuzan," Goo, Grand Sumo, http://sumo.goo.ne.jp/eng/ozumo_meikan/rikishi_joho/rikishi.php?A=38 (accessed 12 July 2005).

50 "'Supermarket' of Wrest[l]ing Tricks," *Mongolia Today*, issue no. 3, http://www..mongoliatoday.com/issue/3/supermarket_tricks.html (accessed 12 July 2005).

51 "Sumo Goes International," Trends in Japan, http://web-japan.org/trends/sports/spo040204.html (accessed 13 July 2005).

52 "Mongolian Wrestler Promoted to Ozeki," *The Japan Times*, July 25, 2002, http://www.japantimes.co.jp/cgi-bin/getarticle.pl5?ss20020725a1.htm (access-

Mongolian sumo wrestler to become a yokozuna, the highest rank in sumo. He was granted the title on January 30, 2003, and is currently the only active yokozuna.[53] Asashoryu was trained as a wrestler by his father from childhood. His father and four brothers are all wrestlers. Asashoryu is relatively light for a sumo wrestler, but he toppled Japanese wrestlers far bigger than himself in spectacular fashion on his way to reaching sumo's pinnacle at the 2003 New Year Grand Sumo Tournament. His success is a matter of great pride for his family and his homeland.[54]

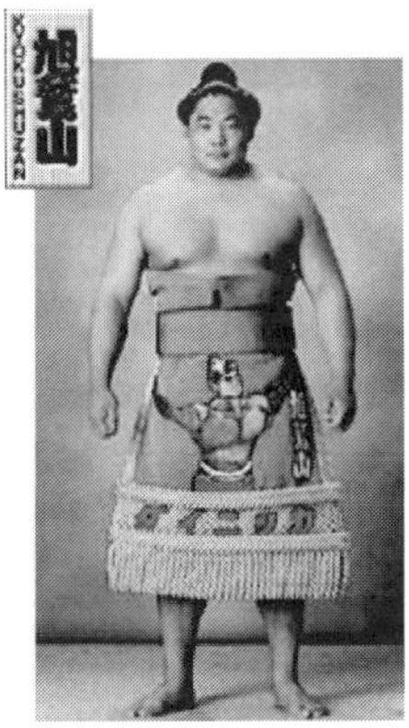

Kyokushuzan D. Batbayar

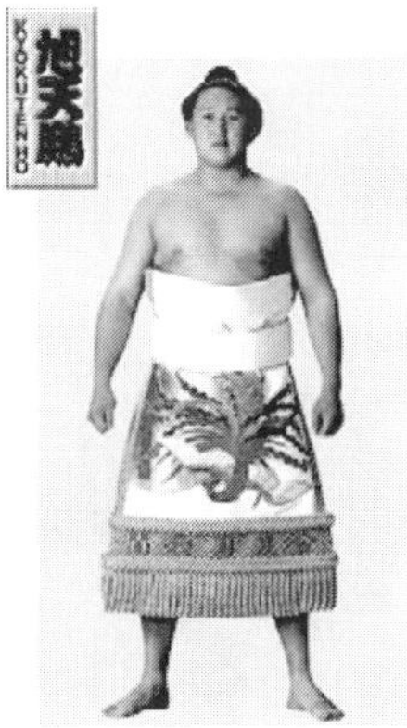

Kyokutenho N. Tsevegnyam

Asashoryu D. Dagvador

As a top national hero, Asashoryu's activities attrack great attention in Mongolia, and it is not surprising to find information about him in the newspapers. During the period that I studied the *UB Post*, I came across many headlines such as "Asashoryu Sets Up Fund for Mongolian Students,"[55]"Asashoryu Completes Formalities: Yokozuna Cruises to Victory Despite Late Upset,"[56] "Asashoryu on Course for Hawaiian Record: Mongolian Set to Take the Plaudits as Sumo's Greatest Foreigner,"[57] "Asashoryu Racks Up Deadly Dozen: Yokozuna Holds Firm to Take Historic Victo-

---

ed 11 July 2005).

53 "Asashōryū Akinori," Wikipedia: The Free Encyclopedia, http://en.wikipedia.org/wiki/Asashoryu (accessed 11 July 2005).

54 "Sumo Goes International."

55 *The UB Post*, 31 March 2005, 5.

56 *The UB Post*, 31 March 2005, 8.

57 *The UB Post*, 19 May 2005, 8.

ry,"[58] and "Asashoryu Wins With Both Mind and Body: Champion Exhibits Mental Grip Over Challengers."[59] After the May sumo tournament, Asashoryu and other Mongolian professional sumo wrestlers arrived in Ulaanbaatar to play basketball against a team of traditional wrestlers. The sumo wrestlers won by a score of 39 to 35. The *UB Post* reported that "basketball league experts said that this game had changed people's understanding of sumo wrestlers, who because of their weight, move very slowly like turtles. Asashoryu, who is the team captain, is 184 cm tall and weighs 145 kg. He scored thirteen points in the game."[60]

Although professional sumo wrestlers, who "are succeeding where their thirteenth century compatriots failed," are the pride of Mongolia, keeping Mongolian citizenship is not always in their personal interest. Kyokutenho N. Tsevegnyam became the first Mongolian wrestler to get Japanese citizenship on June 22, 2005. This enabled him to stay in the sumo world after he retires and become a sumo elder. His fellow Mongol and stablemate Kyokutenzan B. Enkhbat followed suit and also became a Japanese citizen.[61] Since neither Mongolia and Japan recognize dual citizenship, the wrestlers who received Japanese citizenship have to give up their Mongolian citizenship. Mongols are probably not happy to see their heroes become foreign citizens, as evidenced by a reader's comment in the *UB Post.* After learning that Tsevegnyam received Japanese citizenship, a Mongolian reader wrote to the editor that "I feel that he is a pretty selfish guy. After all, who cares about him. He is not good. Get out of here…"[62] In an era of glo-

---

58 *The UB Post*, 26 May 2005, 8.

59 *The UB Post*, 1 June 2005, 8.

60 "Sumo vs Tradition in Famous Names Basketball Game," *The UB Post*, 1 June 2005, 8.

61 "Mongolian Obtains Citizenship," *The Japan Times*, June 26, 2005, http://www.japantimes.co.jp/cgi-bin/getsp.pl5?sp20050626a1.htm; "Sumo Wrestler Tsevegnyam Obtains Japanese Citizenship," *The UB Post*, June 29, 2005, http://ubpost.mongolnews.mn/index.php?subaction=showfull&id=1120042576&archive=&start_from=&ucat=10& (accessed 11 July 2005).

62 A reader's comment to "Sumo Wrestler Tsevegnyam Obtains Japanese Citizenship," in http://ubpost.mongolnews.mn/index.php?subaction=showfull&id=1120042576&archive=&start_from=&ucat=10& (accessed 11 July 2005). When I rechecked the news on November 19, I found this comment removed.

balization, foreign citizenship is welcome by many Mongols even though they are still proud of being Mongols, but for many others traditional pride and practical gain are not always compatible.

CONCLUSION

From the evidence provided by the *UB Post* in the short period of four months, we can clearly see the enormous impact of globalization on the life of the Mongols. They have begun to learn English, Japanese, and Korean, the languages of what they perceive as model countries. Chinese has also become more useful and popular. Thousands of Mongols are working or studying in China, Japan, and South Korea, and many more wish to do so. Mongolian wrestlers have begun to join sumo wrestling in Japan and have brought something new to the sport. Within a little bit more than a decade, they have created a praiseworthy record and become themselves heroes among many Mongols and sumo fans. In addition to languages and sumo, cuisines from other cultures have entered Mongolia and diversified the diet of the Mongols. While shamanism and Buddhism are recovering their hold in Mongolia after a hiatus of more than sixty years, Christianity has also returned, this time as a symbol of the modern developed West. The well-known Mongolian principle of religious tolerance seems to have revived. On the down side, Mongolia's wider opening to the rest of the world has also resulted in some decidedly negative phenomena the worst of which are prostitution and the trafficking of women. Although declared illegal and roundly condemned as immoral, they have become a common practice in Mongolia.

These new developments signify not only language, diet, job, or religious diversification, but a change of value system and identity as well. During the Soviet era, the Mongols were proud of their country as the first socialist country in Asia and a country that "jumped into socialism, bypassing capitalism." They did not consider Mongolia poor because it is a vast country of 1,565,000 square kilometers with a sparse human population and a vast number of herds. However, when Mongolia began its political and economic reforms in the early 1990s, the Mongols suddenly realized that their country is neither big nor rich. I have heard on many occasions some Mongols say that Mongolia is a poor or even a small country. Since Mongolia has chosen a new road of democracy and market economy, its new role models are the West, Japan, and the so-called four Asian tigers, i.e. South Korea, Taiwan, Hong Kong, and Singapore. While old people remain somewhat conservative, many even missing the "good old days," the younger generations in Mongolia are very flexible and ready to exploit any opportunity to reach out to the world. They may be still proud of the glorious past of their ancestors, but they are pragmatic and looking to the future. They are writing a new history of their own.

Unlike anti-globalization protesters in other countries, Mongols seem not to worry too much about the impact of globalization. On the contrary, reading the news and articles in the *UB Post*, one gets the impression that Mongols welcome globalization and are happy to go with the flow. They want to be part of the modern world. However, whether globalization is a blessing or a curse for Mongolia is worth further discussion.[63] The Mongols may be too optimistic or too naive about what globalization will bring them. It is true that globalization is not a new thing. It happened before in history, and the active agents of globalization have often been located far from the West.[64] The Mongol empire was an agent of this kind in the thirteenth century. However, it is also true that the active agents of the current process of globalization are mainly the Western countries. Therefore, this new form of globalization is largely and unavoidably a process of economic, political, and cultural Westernization. Throughout much of the twentieth century Mongolia had undergone a process of Westernization through Soviet influences, but it was very different from today's kind. Mongolia is now a relatively poor country coping with great social changes and uncertainties due to its political and economic transformation. With the inclusion of globalization as a variable to the

---

[63][Editor's note: See Paul D. Buell and Ngan Le's chapter in this book].

[64] Amartya Sen, "Does Globalization Equal Westernization?" *The Globalist*, March 25, 2002, http://www.theglobalist.com/DBWeb/StoryId.aspx?StoryId=2353 (accessed 15 July 2005).

still vulnerable infrastructure, Mongolia without a solid social base will face more difficulties ahead. Since the Mongols have demonstrated their wisdom in the process of post-communist democratization, we expect them to eventually reach a socially acceptable balance between economic prosperity and social justice.

BIBLIOGRAPHY

"About Mongolia," Embassy of Mongolia, Washington D.C. In http://www.mongolianembassy.us/eng_about_mongolia/land_and_people.php (accessed 26 June 2005).

"All Sumo Foreign Rikishi," http://moti.sumogames.com/tForeigners.htm (accessed 11 July 2005).

"Appeal Against Latin Alphabet," *The UB Post*, 3 March 2005, 1.

"Asashōryū Akinori," *Wikipedia : The Free Encyclopedia*, http://en.wikipedia.org/wiki/Asashoryu (accessed 11 July 2005).

"Asashoryu Completes Formalities: Yokozuna Cruises to Victory Despite Late Upset," *The UB Post*, 31 March 2005, 8.

"Asashoryu on Course for Hawaiian Record: Mongolia Set to Take the Plaudits as Sumo's Greatest Foreigner," *The UB Post*, 19 May 2005, 8.

"Asashoryu Racks up Deadly Dozen: Yokozuna Holds Firm to Take Historic Victory," *The UB Post*, 26 May 2005, 8.

"Asashoryu Sets Up Fund for Mongolian Students," *The UB Post*, 31 March 2005, 5.

"Asashoryu Wins With Both Mind and Body: Champion Exhibits Mental Grip Over Challengers," *The UB Post*, 1 June 2005, 8.

Ba, Howie. "The Chinese Are Coming, the Chinese Are Coming." *The UB Post*, 26 May 2005, 8.

"Background Note: Mongolia," U.S. Department of State, http://www.state. gov/r/pa/ei/bgn/2779.htm (accessed 26 June 2005).

Bacon, Paul. "Nomin Talst Play Seoul Music." *The UB Post*, 17 February, 2005, 6.

Batchimeg, Migeddorj. "Future Challenges for the PRC and Mongolia: A Mongolian Perspective." The Jamestown Foundation, http://jamestown.org/publications_details.php?volume_id=40

8&issue_id=3322&article_id=2369704 (accessed 27 June 2005).

Center for Human Rights and Development. "Combating Human Trafficking in Mongolia: Issues and Opportunities." Ulaanbaatar 2003-2004, http://www.asiafoundation.org/pdf/Mongolia-trafficking.pdf (accessed 6 July 2005).

"Curriculum." International School of Ulaanbaatar, http://www.isumongolia.org/index.php?option=content&task=blogcategory&id=12&Itemid=38 (accessed 1 December 2005).

"Database: Inspiring Mongolia," Mongolian National Chamber of Commerce and Industry, http://www.mongolchamber.mn/en/modules.php?name=News&file=article&sid=110 (accessed 11 July 2005).

"Detroit American Bar," *The UB Post*, 26 May 2005, 4.

"English Language Competition Fosters International Connections," *The UB Post*, 9 June 2005, 2.

"English Praise and Worship Evening," *The UB Post*, 19 May 2005, 2.

Freedom House, http://www.freedomhouse.org/research/pressurvey.htm (accessed 23 June 2005)

"Gambare Nippon! Native Sumo Subjugated by Foreign Conquerors," *The UB Post*, 3 February 2005, 8.

"Girls as Sex Workers: Situation and Trends in Mongolia," Gender Center for Sustainable Development, http://www.wirc.mn/research/page4.htm (accessed 3 July 2005).

"Hope Dental Clinic," *The UB Post*, February 8 to April 21, 2005.

"Increase in Korean Air Flights," *The UB Post*, 7 April, 2005, 1.

"International School of Ulaanbaatar," *The UB Post*, February 17 (p. 4), May 5 (p. 3), May 12 (p. 5), May 19 (p. 5), June 1 (p. 3), and June 8 (p. 5) of 2005.

Irra, Isabela. "A Piece of the Middle East." *The UB Post*, 21 April 2005, 7.

"Juvenile Justice in Mongolia," 13, UNICEF–Mongolia, http://mirror.undp.org/mongolia/publications/JJ_Eng.pdf (accessed 6 July 2005).

Kholl, Moe. "Help, I'm Locked Inside a Chinese Cookie Factory." *The UB Post*, 28 April 2005, 7.

"Komodo Village," *The UB Post*, 21 April 2005, 7.

"Kyokushuzan," Goo, Grand Sumo, http://sumo.goo.ne.jp/

eng/ozumo_meikan/rikishi_joho/rikishi.php?A=38 (accessed 12 July 2005).

"Le Bistrot Francais," *The UB Post*, 3 March 2005, 3.

"Learning as an International Experience: Canadian Project Crosses Borders in Education," *The UB Post*, 1 June 2005, 5.

Ma, Ho-t'ien. *Chinese Agent in Mongolia : A Report on the Birth of the Mongolian People's Republic.* Translated by John De Francis. Baltimore: The Johns Hopkins Press, 1949.

"Mongolia," Country Reports on Human Rights Practices–2002, U.S. Department of State, http://www.state.gov/g/drl/rls/hrrpt/2002/18255.htm (accessed 4 July 2005).

"Mongolia," Country Reports on Human Rights Practices–2004, U.S. Department of State, http://www.state.gov/g/drl/rls/hrrpt/2004/41652.htm (accessed 3 July 2005).

"Mongolia," Federal Foreign Office of Germany, http://www.auswaertigesamt.de/www/en/laenderinfos/laender/laender_ausgabe_html?type_id=14&land_id=115(accessed 27 June 2005).

"Mongolia," Serving in Mission, http://www.sim.co.uk/where/mongolia.htm (accessed 27 June 2005).

"Mongolian Catholics Rejoice for Pope Benedict XVI," *The UB Post*, 28 April 2005, 1.

"Mongolian Obtains Citizenship," *The Japan Times*, June 26, 2005, http://www.japantimes.co.jp/cgi-bin/getsp.pl5?sp20050626a1.htm(accessed 11 July 2005).

"Mongolian Wrestler Promoted to Ozeki," *The Japan Times*, July 25, 2002, http://www.japantimes.co.jp/cgi-bin/getarticle.pl5?ss 20 020725a1.htm (accessed 11 July 2005).

National Human Rights Commission of Mongolia and Center for Human Rights and Development. "The Crime of Trafficking of Women and Children in Mongolia: The Current Situation." (Ulaanbaatar, November 2002), 9, http://www.owc.org.mn/chrd/publication/Trafficking%20Report%202002-eng.doc (accessed 4 July 2005).

"One-Hour Non-Stop Praise and Worship," *The UB Post*, 9 June 2005, 4.

Park, James Brown. "Seoul Food." *The UB Post*, 9 June 2005, 8.

"People Trafficking on the Rise," *The Mongol Messenger*, http://

www.mongol messenger.mn/issue/040207.php (accessed 6 July 2005).
Po[e]psel, Iryna. "A Hunger for Russian Food." *The UB Post*, 3 February 2005, 7.
________. "Italian Cuisine in Ulaanbaatar." *The UB Post*, 10 March 2005, 7.
________. "Korean Gem Hidden in Deepest Bayanzurkh." *The UB Post*, 17 February 2005, 8.
________. "No. 5: Kotletas." *The UB Post*, 24 February 2005, 8.
"President Sends Telegram to the Vatican," *The UB Post*, 7 April 2005, 1.
Sen, Amartya. "Does Globalization Equal Westernization?" *The Globalist*, March 25, 2002, http://www.theglobalist.com/DB Web/StoryId.aspx?StoryId =2353 (accessed 15 July 2005).
Smith, Todd. "No. 9: Aglio e Olio." *The UB Post*, 21 April 2005, 7.
"Sumo Goes International," Trends in Japan, http://web-japan.org/trends/sports/spo040204.html (accessed 13 July 2005).
"A Sumo Pioneer," *Kansai Time Out* 333 (November 2004), http://www.kto.co.jp/2004nov/article4.html (accessed 12 July 2005).
"Sumo vs Tradition in Famous Names Basketball Game," *The UB Post*, 1 June 2005, 8.
"Sumo Wrestler Tsevegnyam Obtains Japanese Citizenship," *The UB Post*, June 29, 2005, http://ubpost.mongolnews.mn/index.php?subaction=showfull&id=1120042576&archive=&start_from=&ucat=10& (accessed 11 July 2005).
"'Supermarket' of Wrest[l]ing Tricks," *Mongolia Today*, issue no. 3, http://www.mongoliatoday.com/issue/3/supermarket_tricks.html (accessed 12 July 2005).
"The Dark Side of Casino Lights," *The UB Post*, 24 March 2005, 4.
"Trip to Illinois Concretes Education," *The UB Post*, 31 March 2005, 5.
"Twelve Mongolians Deported from South Korea," *The UB Post*, 8 February, 2005, 5.
"Ulaanbaatar Elite International School," *The UB Post*, April 28 (p. 3), May 5 (p. 5), May 12 (p. 5), May 19 (p. 5), May 26 (p. 3), June 1 (p. 6), and June 8 (p. 3), 2005.
"Ulaanbaatar MK School," *The UB Post*, 26 May 2005, 5.

Global Hip-Hop and Youth Cultural Politics in Urban Mongolia

Peter K. Marsh

One of the most geographically remote nations in the world, Mongolia has been affected by many of the same cultural flows that have transformed youth culture throughout the world during the twentieth century. Since the 1960s, the nation's youth have been in contact with various forms of Western commercial popular music. When hip-hop emerged from the Bronx in the 1980s, it spread throughout the United States and then on to other nations. It took root in Mongolia as well, arriving in the mid- to late 1990s. Since the early 2000s it has become one of the most important mainstream musical and cultural forms.

On the surface, the progress of rap and hip-hop culture from New York City to Ulaanbaatar appears simply to be the result of the forces of globalization, the integration of capitalist markets that allows the free movement of commodities from one part of the world to another. Yet as Appadurai reminds us, the process is considerably more complex, involving the movement of people, money, ideas, media and technology—all of which are "fluid, overlapping, and disjunctive"[1] in ways in which no one dimension is paramount over nor controlled by any one monolithic entity or system. But when dealing with complex cultural forms, it is important to ask not only *what* is being created but also *how* it is being re-

[1] Arjun Appadurai, "Disjunctures and Difference in the Global Cultural Economy," *Public Culture* 2:2 (1990), 7.

ceived. While both Mongolia and the United States have hip-hop cultures, the different ways each of them is conceived can help us to better understand Mongolia's relationship with the processes of cultural globalization.

This study examines the development of hip-hop in the context of an emerging popular music industry in Mongolia over the period of approximately forty years. From this perspective, hip-hop appears to be no mere imitative or derivative form of Western popular music, but rather one that has been skillfully appropriated by media-saturated Mongolian youths and adapted to specific conditions of their local context in urban Ulaanbaatar, Mongolia's sprawling and densely populated capital city. While Mongolian hip-hop bears clear similarities with the 'gangsta' rap traditions of the United States, a closer look shows that it is much more abstract than may at first be apparent. Tricia Rose has offered valuable frameworks for the study of hip-hop within African American contexts, but the studies by scholars such as Tony Mitchell and Ian Maxwell, who have examined hip-hop outside of the United States, offer especially useful sources for this analysis. While Mongolian rappers are interacting with the transnational hip-hop scene, they are also responding to the popular musical scene in their own nation in ways that are rich with new ideas about being young and Mongolian in contemporary Mongolia.

WESTERN-INSPIRED POPULAR MUSIC

Western-inspired popular music genres have a long history in Mongolia. Russian and Soviet forms of popular culture were introduced to the country following the People's Revolution of 1921, which soon brought Mongolia into the orbit of the Soviet Union. Throughout the twentieth century, genres such as circus and film music, ballroom dance, and jazz held an important place in the newly developed national media, a network of newspapers, radio, film, and (later) television that the state expanded into the farthest reaches of the Mongolian countryside. Other important forms of popular culture included professional folk music, music theatre, and a uniquely Mongolian form of popular song known as "composed" songs (*zokhiolyn duu*).[2] Each of these genres was integrated into the nation's newly developed schools of music and closely controlled by state-run cultural organizations, often in close cooperation with musicians, composers, and producers from the Soviet Union.

Restrictions on travel and trade that were maintained by the Soviet-backed ruling party, the Mongolian People's Revolutionary Party (MPRP), effectively isolated the country from the cultural influences of nations outside of the Soviet world. But even so, by the 1960s, elements of the mainstream musical culture of the non-Soviet West began to find their way into the hands of Mongolian youths. These included vinyl LP records and recorded audio tapes featuring the music of the Beatles, the Rolling Stones, Led Zeppelin, Smokie and other Western popular music groups of the late 1960s and early 1970s, which were often smuggled into the country in their luggage by the children of Mongolian diplomats posted abroad or musicians returning from foreign tours. These cultural materials were then circulated in decidedly illicit ways, frequently passing among youths (primarily in Ulaanbaatar) through hand-to-hand networks, not unlike those described by Ryback[3] and others in parts of the former Soviet Union. Many Mongolian youths were fascinated with the new sounds that these groups were creating and the new forms of youth culture they represented. A thriving underground market in popular material culture grew up in the period, which beyond musical recordings included the distribution of Western styles of clothing (particularly blue jeans), magazines, posters, and jewelry.

At first suspicious of this music and the global or "capitalist" systems that had brought it to the doorstep of their nation, the

---

[2] *Zokhiolyn duu* is a hybrid genre featuring newly composed melodies that are modeled after folk song melodies and accompanied by small ensembles or orchestras.

[3] Timothy Ryback, *Rock Around the Bloc : A History of Rock Music in Eastern Europe and the Soviet Union* (New York: Oxford University Press, 1990); see also S. Frederick Starr, *Red and Hot : The Fate of Jazz in the Soviet Union* (New York: Oxford University Press, 1983); Artemy Troitsky, *Back in the USSR* (London: Faber and Faber, 1987); and Sabrina Petra Ramet, ed., *Rocking the State* (Boulder: Westview Press, 1994).

leaders in the MPRP soon came to realize that they could not stop this movement of Western material culture by banning it or violently suppressing it. Thus they chose to appropriate it into the national culture, but on the Party's own terms. Starting in the early 1970s, the Party formed and managed a number of so-called *estrad* ensembles (the Russian word for staged entertainment), two of the first being Cultural Jewel (*Soyol Erdene*) and Rich Mongolia (*Bayan Mongol*).

These were groups of Mongolian artists performing Western-inspired popular music in a "socialist" style. While Cultural Jewel on-stage--with a drummer, one to two electric guitarists, a bassist and a lead singer--resembled its Western counterparts, the cultural setting in which the group worked was entirely different. As a state-managed ensemble, this and other such ensembles were assigned specific places within a hierarchy of other state-run organizations directly linked to the Ministry of Culture. The Party provided them with regular salaries, access to musical instruments and training, and organized regular concerts, recording opportunities, and tours throughout the Mongolian countryside and to other socialist "brother" nations. In exchange, these artists and groups had to go where the Party wanted them to go and to do what it wanted them to do: they were expected to wear the stage uniforms the Party created for them, to perform the repertoire the Party gave them, and even to cut their hair as the Party directed.

By the 1980s *estrad* music formed an important part of the nation's cultural mainstream. Especially popular were sentimental love ballads and those that drew upon more traditional themes, such as songs that praised the beauty of the Mongolian landscape. Artists were also provided with songs that glorified the nation's development and the wisdom of the Soviet leaders. But the Party's official legitimation of Western-inspired popular music proved to be a double-edged sword as artists increasingly began to challenge the Party's authority to control the entire political and artistic space within the realm of popular culture. In the mid-1980s the lead singer of the group Cultural Jewel, D. Jargalsaikhan, felt that the time was right to defy Party rules and sing a song he had written about Chinggis Khan, a subject that was still largely considered to be taboo in public discussion. The song praised the spirit of the great khan, asking him to forgive the Mongolian people for forgetting about him for so many years. In singing it at a public concert, Jargalsaikhan was not only expressing his deep convictions about this powerful symbol of Mongolian identity, but also playing to the growing nationalist sentiments of his Mongolian listeners.

The band Bell (*Khonkh*) also played an important role in this regard. It was led by two young Mongolian classmates who had just returned from journalism school in Russia. The group's most famous song, "Sound of the Bell" (*Khonkhny duu*), calls on people to wake up to the dawning of a new day. Its melody was taken up and sung by protesters during the street demonstrations and protest rallies that took place outside government buildings between 1989 and 1990.

The group Khonkh performing during one of the pre-democracy protest rallies in 1990. *Courtesy Peter K. Marsh*

Another of the group's very popular songs depicts the confusion, if not desperation, of Party members who are watching the growing political protests from their office windows:

The city looks very beautiful. If you look through the window,

> *people walk purposefully on the streets. Through the window, life seems pleasant. Send a message, girl: All is fine, all is right. Please take this down, write it down. Tell them not to demand any more.*[4]

The song resonated with a widespread sense of unease about a national leadership that many felt to be out of touch with the everyday lives and problems of its citizens. Its popularity also reflected the rise of an independent-minded generation of artists who sought to claim the realm of popular culture for themselves. Mongolian *estrad* groups were no longer merely imitating their Western idols nor passively glorifying state ideology. They instead had mastered their Western genres and the technical skills needed to produce them and were increasingly appropriating them to speak to the situations in which they found themselves. The important role that the group Bell played in helping to focus the sentiments of the pro-democracy demonstrators demonstrated the emerging maturity and growing authority that popular music was attaining in the period, trends that would continue without pause into the post-socialist era.

MONGOLIAN POP FINDS ITS OWN VOICE

Popular music around the time of the so-called democratic revolution of 1990 was frequently rife with political ideas and criticism. This was a time, Jargalsaikhan says, "when politics was in the air we breathed."[5] But following the rapid introduction of market economic reforms and the successful completion of the nation's first multi-party election, youth interest in politics faded fast. A contributing factor for this was the severe economic downturn that accompanied the sudden end to generous Soviet subsidies, coupled with the economic shock therapy advocated by the World Bank. Mongols suddenly faced not only the disappearance of many social services they had come to rely upon, but also a steep de-

---

[4] Nicholas D. Kristof, "A Mongolian Rock Group Fosters Democracy," *The New York Times* (26 March 1990), C11:1.

[5] Jargalsaikhan, in 1999 interview.

cline in their living standards. For many in this period, even finding enough food to eat was difficult. Mongols had finally won the right to speak their minds and to travel freely, although few had the resources to do so.

Despite the difficult economic situation (and likely in part because of it), Mongolian popular culture expanded dramatically in the first half of the 1990s, fueled in large part by the sudden availability of communication and recording technologies. Several new independent media and broadcasting companies began operations in Ulaanbaatar, including a number of privately owned television and FM radio stations, bringing real competition to the still state-run and still largely centralized Montsame news service and Mongolian Radio & Television. Satellite and cable TV entered the market by the mid-1990s and quickly gained popularity in the urban areas. Some of the more popular ones included the MTV and MTV-Asia channels. Computer centers also began to open around the city that offered Mongols access to computer games and the Internet as well as to training in how to build websites and use advanced computer software. Such developments gave Mongolian youths for the first time direct access to the transnational flows of popular culture. At the same time, young people were gaining access to relatively inexpensive technologies that allowed them to record, mix, and master audio and video recordings, which in turn allowed them to begin creating their own songs and videos at levels of quality and control that were unavailable to earlier generations of popular musical artists. These new technologies allowed artists to not only consume the "global" popular music but also interact with it at a local level.

Mongolian popular music itself became increasingly diverse throughout the 1990s as artists began to experiment with the new genres that they were hearing in the international media, including pop ballads, boy and girl bands, and rock music. Some of the most famous artists included the pop singers Jargalsaikhan, Sarantuya, and Ariunaa (who has been dubbed the 'Madonna of Mongolia'); boy bands like Camerton and girl bands like the Spike Girls. Hurd and Kharanga also achieved a great deal of popularity as "heavy metal" and "hard rock" groups, respectively. While these performers were usually inspired by well-known Western artists and groups, each developed their own unique musical and presentational styles.

Typically, few popular musical artists perform cover versions of Western popular music since most say that Mongolian audiences prefer their artists to create uniquely Mongolian forms of these Western genres. For the artists, this means finding a stylistic balance between the two. As in the socialist era, songs about finding love and happiness have continued to be favored song themes. But many artists have also continued to draw upon traditional themes, such as love for one's parents, the beauty of the Mongolian landscape, or the wonders of the Mongolian horse. It is common for artists to create songs that blend the sounds of traditional Mongolian folk musical instruments and singing styles. At the same time, they have also become quite sophisticated at understanding the wishes of their audiences, and many are wary of moving too far towards the "traditional." The members of the rock band Hurd explained to me that most bands have two kinds of song repertoires. For audiences consisting of foreigners or older generations of Mongols they perform songs that are "more traditional" or that romanticize Mongolian culture, but for their young Mongolian fans, they perform songs that are instead closely inspired by the Western rock bands they idolize, which for Hurd means songs styled after the famous heavy metal bands Black Sabbath and AC/DC.[6]

Since at least the middle of the twentieth century, Mongolian popular music has followed cultural trends that we can call cosmopolitan.[7] By the 1970s, the ruling MPRP insisted that its artists produce uniquely Mongolian forms of music that could stand as "Mongolian" contributions to the much larger Soviet "international" world of popular music. In this way, Mongolian artists have been dealing with the issues of the globalization of popular music for decades, although the "global" in this sense was limited to the world of the Soviet Union and its satellites. In the post-socialist era, Mongols have continued to create hybrid forms of popular

---

[6] Hurd, in 1999 interview.

[7] Cf. Marsh for a discussion of cosmopolitan cultural trends in Mongolian music.

music that is fashioned after Western popular song genres and yet uniquely Mongolian in sound and style. When Mongols ask foreign visitors how their music compares with Western popular music, one gets the sense that they would like to hear their music compared seriously with the "best of the West."

GROWTH OF A POP MUSIC INDUSTRY IN THE 1990s

By the late 1990s, popular musical artists were not only beginning to find their own individual voices, but also to conceive of themselves as a distinct community. When the Mongolian government declared 1998 to be the "Year of the Youth," a year-long celebration of Mongolia's young people and their potential, many of the leading Mongolian popular music artists of the day gathered to sing the song commissioned by the government for the event, "The future begins today" (*Ireedui onoodroos ekhelnee*). The song was structured in a way that allowed individual artists and groups to take turns singing verses, with short musical breaks made to accommodate changes in genre style; the chorus refrain was then sung by all the performers in unison. The artists lined up on stage in a long row, stepping forward into the spotlight to sing their own verse. The song and its accompanying video proved to be very popular with people throughout the nation and they were subsequently broadcast on local and national FM radio and television broadcasts throughout the year. The song's overall effect was to present a musical community that, despite its diversity of individual styles, was united in its goal of celebrating the nation's youth, not unlike the effect the 1985 song "We Are the World" had in uniting leading Euro-American singers toward the goal of fighting hunger in Africa.

Other important steps toward founding and unifying this community involved the creation of organizations that helped to legitimize its practices. The establishment in 1997 of an annual year-end music awards ceremony called Pentatonic, which its organizers now market as the "Mongolian Grammys," allows this emerging industry to recognize and reward the performers, producers, and production companies that have achieved popular success within it. This is a process that, as with its American counterpart, has helped to define the popular musical mainstream in Mongolia. The formation of the Mongolian Singer's Union (*Mongolyn duuchny kholboo*) in 1998 has also assisted in this process. The organization seeks to organize professional singers throughout the nation, to lobby the government on important issues (their efforts contributed to the Ulaanbaatar city government's decision to build the multi-stage "UB Palace" in 2002), and to assist singers in the countryside.[8]

The increasingly formalized ways in which the business of popular music was run in this period was encouraged in large part by the young industry's growing ties with big business. By the late 1990s, popular artists and bands were finding eager sponsors from among many of the new emerging businesses of post-socialist Mongolia, including luxury clothing (principally cashmere wool) manufacturers; alcoholic breweries (principally the several highly successful joint ventures between German and Mongolian beer manufacturers established in the period in Ulaanbaatar), importers and upper-class bars; and luxury car distributors (the local Mercedes-Benz distributor was one of the most generous). Other important sponsors included media companies that were, in this period, in the process of consolidating into a few large private entities. Since then they have come to control most of the important radio and television stations and national and urban newspapers. These sponsors financially supported artists in the production of their CDs and music-videos and the organization of their concerts and tours. In turn they benefited from their name association with those that became successful. An extreme example of this came in the late 1990s when the popular heavy metal band Hurd signed a sponsorship deal with the Erel Company of Mongolia, one of the largest of the domestic mining companies. Soon thereafter the band was renamed Erel-Hurd.

The presence of these sponsors also points to a deeper social transformation that has been occurring in Ulaanbaatar since the mid-1990s. Though a large percentage of Mongols continue to live

---

[8] Hurd and Jargalsaikhan, in their 1999 interviews.

in relative poverty,[9] the overall growth of the national economy in the past decade has helped many achieve a higher standard of living. Mining, tourism and trade are just some of the major new sectors of the nation's economy. The recent boom in the markets for new apartments, cars, and electronic goods in Ulaanbaatar is a sign of an emerging middle class with cash to spend on goods, luxuries, and entertainment. Mongolian popular musical artists have found many new venues to perform with the opening of night clubs and bars that cater to the middle and upper classes. The "classless" society that was said to exist during the socialist era is now becoming increasingly divided between the relatively rich and poor sectors of society.[10] While there are many who are benefiting from the new opportunities in the Mongolian economy, particularly Mongolian entrepreneurs and the highly educated, there are many more who are not or cannot, particularly those in the public sector. Even university professors and medical doctors working in public institutions continue to earn an average of $100 a month in salary, and often less in the countryside.

The relative appearance of wealth in Ulaanbaatar, however, continues to be a driving force in the rising number of people who are migrating from rural areas to the capital city, where most seek jobs and the services and amenities located there.[11] Many, however, end up in the sprawling *ger* districts on the edges of the city. These are named after the traditional round tents (*gers*) in which nomadic herder families live in the countryside. Many new immigrants to the city set up their *ger*s and surround them with a wooden fence, making a small family compound (*khashaa*) that is attached to other such compounds. Many of the residencies in

---

[9] The latest measurements by the United Nations Development Programmes state that 35.6% of the population in 1998 was living below the poverty line (UNDP 2003: 12).

[10] The UNDP found that the Gini-coefficient, a measure of income inequality, increased by 42% between 1995 and 1998, showing "that the income distribution is becoming more unequal in Mongolia" (UNDP 2003: 26).

[11] Joerg Janzen and his co-workers found that most people immigrated to the city from rural areas in search of an improved standard of living and better access to employment, medical services and schools. See their *A New Ger-Settlement in Ulaanbaatar: Functional Differentiation, Demographic and Socioeconomic Structure and Origin of Residents* (Ulaanbaatar, 2002), 18.

these districts lack electricity and running water, and other social services like schools and medical clinics are in short supply. Most families living there sold their domesticated animals before coming to the city with the hope that they would find jobs to support themselves, but levels of unemployment in these districts remain high, as do levels of crime. Despite the population density and high levels of poverty, the *ger* districts are not widely considered to be ghettos or slums among Mongols in Ulaanbaatar, as similar places might be in other parts of the world. But there is a growing stigma among wealthier city residents towards those who live in some of these districts. Popular musicians, for their part, remain well aware that many of their fans come from poor households, whether or not they live in the *ger* districts, and thus they try to keep the costs of their concert tickets and CDs low, typically around US$3 to $5 a piece.

Another sign of the growing influence of mainstream popular music is the close relationships that exist between artists and leading politicians and political parties. Political leaders are well aware of the potential political power of popular music. More than a few in the current generation might even have participated in the public demonstrations more than a decade ago. In each of the national elections for both the Parliament and Presidency since the late 1990s, the main political parties have drafted popular music artists into their campaigns; some demanding that artists sign contracts that require them to work exclusively for a specific political party. The appearance of pop stars and groups at campaign rallies and in political campaign advertising has become a common part of the political scene in contemporary Mongolia. Some artists have even begun to actively campaign in support of particular candidates and parties, sometimes even composing campaign theme songs.

Mongolian youths of the past several decades have shown themselves to be keen observers of Western and "global" popular cultural styles and fully capable of appropriating and adapting them to their own musical and artistic worlds. Since the late 1980s popular musical artists have taken advantage of the economic, political, and technological changes that have come to Mongolia and established the basis for a powerful popular music industry. Popular music in this country has developed hand-in-glove with emerging entities in the worlds of the mass media, business, and politics, each "scratching the other's back." This industry also has grown in parallel with an emerging middle class in Ulaanbaatar. It is now as integrated with the nation's superculture as it was at the height of the socialist era, one difference being that now many of the formerly rebellious youths who chafed against the Party's attempts to control their art are themselves its representatives, and like the Party leaders they served, these industry leaders have much at stake in maintaining its conventions. But as in youth cultures throughout the world, where one finds accommodation to mainstream authority, one will typically also find subcultural resistance to it. In the late 1990s and early 2000s, "*rep*" and "*hip hop*", terms the Mongols themselves use, have emerged as both a reaction against the conventions of the popular musical mainstream and expressions of self-identity from a new generation of Mongols seeking to make their voice heard in the youth cultural scene.

RAPPERS AS THE 'BAD BOYS' OF THE MUSICAL WORLD

The first popular group to rap in their music was Black Rose (*Khar Sarnai*). The group, consisting of two brothers, burst onto the scene in the early 1990s with their loud, raw, and beat-heavy music, wild hair, face paints, fantastic costumes, and vigorous dancing. Describing their music as "techno-rap," the two singers commonly traded raps with each other over heavy house beats. The pair would often shout their lyrics at their audience in guttural and growling voices. Their songs were typically fast-paced and on stage the duo would constantly move about and dance, thrusting their fists and legs into the air. While many of their songs dealt with love, the duo described them as love songs that were "more realistic" than those common to the mainstream ballad singers. Their songs also often touched on taboo themes: one early hit for the group described a man's love for a prostitute.

In their musical, lyrical and presentational style, Black Rose signaled a clear break from the refined, well-quaffed and well-behaved ballad singers who dominated the musical mainstream throughout the era of socialism and into the 1990s. In challenging the Mongolian pop song conventions of the day, the group was seeking to clear a space for a new subcultural musical style. Although influenced by the Western "techno" and "rap" artists they had experienced through the media, they sought to create and market a new musical voice that they felt to be particularly well suited to the cultural and political landscape of their homeland.

The "techno-rap" group Black Rose (Black Rose 2001).

The duo described themselves in the late 1990s as nationalists who wanted their music and dance to instill within young Mongols a feeling of pride in their nation, its history, and traditions. They accomplished this by actively mixing Mongolian folk musical, song and dance traditions and traditional song themes with hip-hop, techno, and house beats. The group's attempts in the late 1990s to establish a nationalist-oriented nationwide youth organization shows that their "play" with these Western cultural forms was also an engagement with the very serious business of cultural politics in the nation in that period. Many hip-hop artists today do not consider Black Rose to be a part of the early history of rap in Mongolia, labeling their style as "techno." But in its popular mixture of music, dance, and performance art, as well as its cultural outspokenness, the group clearly did help a rising generation of Mongolian performers to conceive of popular music in new ways.

The group Tatar (Tatar n.d.).

A number of self-described *rep* groups had formed by the late-1990s, but it was not until the early 2000s that the genre really began to catch the public's eye. Most of the first groups to gain popularity then, including Digital, Ice Top, Montarep, Lumino, and Tatar, remain some of the most popular and established groups today, though there are now at least ten other groups working in Ulaanbaatar. Of these only one, 3 Girls (*3 Okhin*), consists of women rappers. In Mongolia, as in other parts of the world, rap is a largely male activity, although women nearly always appear as back-up singers on recordings and supporting actresses in videos. The Mongolian artists interviewed for this study were quick to list the international artists and groups that inspired them, some of the more influential being Eminem, Tupac Shakur, Snoop Doggy Dogg, MC Hammer, and Wu-Tang Clan, as well as some well-known non-American groups like the French rappers MC Solaar and IAM and even a number of South Korean and Japanese rap groups.

Through their "street" clothing, body movements and gestures, jewelry and forms of bodily ornamentation, Mongolian rappers and hip-hop artists show their allegiance to their idols as well as their determination to bring hip-hop to Mongolia in their own unique ways. They also show the degree to which they are interacting with the master narratives about the origins and development of hip-hop that have accompanied the song form to the country. Tricia Rose writes that as hip-hop spread and took root in different parts of the United States, it retained the "larger forces that define hip-hop and Afrodiasporic cultures," including its articulation of "a sense of entitlement and pleasure in aggressive insubordination."[12] That Mongolian rappers have eagerly taken up this sense of entitlement and insubordination is evident in most of their rap concerts, videos, websites, CDs and other forms of public display.

For example, many revel in "gangsta" or "bad boy" imagery. Like their international counterparts, Mongolian rappers prefer "street thug" clothing, typically ranging from loose-fitting sports-

[12] Tricia Rose, *Black Noise: Rap Music and Black Culture in Contemporary America* (Middletown: Wesleyan University Press, 1994), 60.

wear (usually bearing the icons of American sports teams) to tight-fitting leather jackets and pants. Many wear large pieces of jewelry, such as rings and chain necklaces, and commonly bare body piercings and tattoos. Most wear baseball caps (worn backward or to the side), but some shave off their hair completely. The rappers bounce and sway to the beats of their music on stage and in their videos, and typically use hand signals and gestures seen in Western rap videos. In each of these ways, Mongolian rappers are both aligning themselves with international hip-hop customs while also

The group Lumino in hip-hop style (Lumino 2003).

defining their style as different from the love ballad, boy band, and rock genres of the Mongolian popular musical mainstream.

The "insubordination" of these Mongolian hip-hop groups extends to their use of obscene language, graffiti, and provocative storylines for their videos and CDs. Mongolian rappers' heavy use of swear words in their lyrics has led to the rise "parental advisory for explicit content" labels[13] similar to those in the United States that artists are required to place onto their CDs. Rather than being ashamed of these labels or hiding them on the back sides of their CDs, however, most groups show them on the fronts of their CDs as if they are badges of honor.

Graffiti has also emerged as another form of insubordination broadly associated with hip-hop in Mongolia. While many instan-

Graffiti images associated with hip-hop groups in downtown Ulaanbaatar.
Courtesy Peter K. Marsh.

ces of graffiti throughout Ulaanbaatar appear to be spontaneous and illicit, such as spray-painting the names of hip-hop groups on the sides of buildings, some of the more significant forms of graf-

---

[13] In Mongolian, *tümend niitsekhüüts khelleg aguulagdaw.*

fiti appear to be meticulously planned. A clear example of the latter is found on a long concrete wall overlooking an unused lot in downtown Ulaanbaatar, just across from the city's central square.

Images associated with six different hip-hop groups have been painted onto the walls in graffiti style. Members of some of these groups said that these groups recently banded together to hire a local artist to make these paintings. One of these paintings, however, is an advertisement for a local sports bar painted in graffiti style, suggesting that they all could have been done with both financial support from local businesses and the approval of local authorities.

In a similar way, groups are often provocative in the images they use to accompany their CDs and songs. In their 2004 CD "New Life," which features the logo of a marijuana leaf, the group Ice Top includes a photographic spread in the liner notes featuring band members dressed as thieves meeting after a heist. While some are counting stacks of American dollar bills, others appear to be sniffing cocaine.

The group Ice Top dressed as thieves (Ice Top n.d.).

In 2002 the Mongolian government tried to stop the airing of a music video of their song "Follow Me and Have Fun" (*Namaig dagaad tsenge*) by the group Lumino. Shot in a strip club, the video featured band members rapping while Mongolian women in thongs lay on tables and danced around them. Soon after its release, the Mongolian Minister of Justice labeled the video "pornographic" and ordered it banned from being broadcast on those television stations closely allied with the ruling political party. As might be expected, the Minister's denunciation helped to boost the sales of the group's CD and enhanced the 'bad boy' image of this and other rap groups. The song eventually became one of the group's biggest hits and went on to win the Best Song of the Year award at the music industry's Pentatonic awards ceremony later that year. The group's re-release of the video in 2004 featured the words "censored" in English flashing on various parts of the screen, as if the group was thumbing its nose at the Minister's attempts to ban it.

Other key elements of global hip-hop that Mongolian rappers have picked up on are the ideas of the "crew" and "neighborhood." Rose explains that American rappers employ the symbolic language of the "ghetto" by referring to their band members as their "crew."[14] She describes crews as a "new kind of families forged with intercultural bonds that … provide insulation and support" not unlike the social networks within gangs.[15] They share a body of codes, from tattoos, piercings, haircut, and clothing styles to body movement and hand gestures that signify their identity as belonging to a particular gang or neighborhood. Mongolian rappers tend not to have as highly defined a system of identity markers, but they do commonly portray themselves as having a "crew," and some even use this word in their band's name.[16] Groups commonly like to portray themselves as a part of a community or neighborhood of friends. One recent video by the young group Snep Crew opens with the artists breakdancing on a street in front of upper-middle class homes in Ulaanbaatar, surrounded and being urged on by their friends sitting nearby on the ground and on parked cars.

The scenes change to an outdoor courtyard where they play basketball, a sports hall where they box, a room in a house where they "scratch" LP records, and an abandoned building where they

---

[14] Rose, *op. cit.,* 10.

[15] *Ibid.*, 34.

[16] "BAT and The Crew" and "Snep Crew" are the best known examples of this practice.

breakdance. The overall image is of a community filled with young people living in one close-knit "neighborhood," all having a good time through dancing, listening to and making music, playing

Breakdancing on the street, from the video "Jin tan" (Snep Crew 2004).

sports, and "hanging out" together. For other rappers, however, the "neighborhood" that their crew passes through has more in common with the stereotypical "hoods" found in Western 'gangsta' rap videos, such as abandoned factory sites, an old train yard, or dilapidated buildings.

Setting their videos in such blighted and post-industrial parts of Ulaanbaatar reflects the wish of many groups to address the darker sides of growing up. Many songs deal with the problems of finding love, creating one's own identity, and figuring out one's own way in the world. While love is a common theme in all popular music, most Mongolian hip-hop songs about love are "harder" and "darker." Many deal with the pain of love, though often from a man's point of view, given that the majority of rappers are male. The song "Someone's" (*Khüniikh*) by the group Lumino features one of the singers rapping to his friends about how he tried to win the heart of the woman he truly loved, only to find out that she "belonged" to someone else.

The group Lumino, from the video "Khüniikh" (Lumino 2003).

A song by the group Digital, "Only One Life to Live" (*Gants l amidarch ükhne*), has the rappers struggling with deeper questions about how one should live one's life:

In life, all people are growing up and falling down,
So what are we to do with our lives?
Some people drink a lot, others study a lot,
But what are they really reaching for?
Life is difficult to understand.[17]

Some groups take this idea of "harder" and "darker" further, seeing hip-hop as a medium for criticizing larger social problems in their society. A number of rappers said they were attracted to hip-hop because of the freedom that the genre gave them to express their ideas, hopes, and fears. While most groups continue to rap about love and the problems of growing up in Mongolia, many do see in hip-hop the opportunity to express their frustrations

[17] Digital, "This Is Life" (2003).

with larger problems in their society. The rapper Batorgil, from the group Ice Top, is clear about this:

> Our society is very dirty[18] and we can easily reveal these things through our hip-hop art. There are many people who are angry and anxious, and we can give them a voice. But pop-rock [singers] always sing about love. Pop-rock cannot raise these problems in our society.

The rapper BAT emphasizes the idea that rap allows people to speak about their world in realistic, rather than romantic, ways:

> On both [of my previous] albums, I rap about the country—and I don't mean about how beautiful it is because we have mountains or whatever. I don't do that. I just speak about what I see, you know. Too many people are asking for money. Too many people are drunk or homeless. And I also talk about what the government, these 76 [parliamentarians], are doing.[19]

There are some groups that have created songs that criticize specific types of bad behavior or difficult situations in Mongolia. In its song "A Growing Flower," the group Digital chastises people for treating street children badly. "Their condition is not their fault," they rap, "their parents are at fault for not thinking about their children's future." The group War & Peace takes on the larger question of the insensitivity of the nation's leaders to the suffering of the poor in its song, "A Letter to Our President":

> *The government spends four years doing nothing. They never do the things they promised. I have seen your smiling face on television and read what you've written, but there is little that you have implemented. Do you run the country from your black glassed windowed cars? From behind the windows, the poor Mongolians won't be seen.*[20]

---

[18] *Bokhir* means dirty but also "not fair or straight" and commonly referring to corruption.

[19] Batbold, in 2005 interview.

[20] Dain ba Enkh, "Neg Chig" (2002).

Such political criticism, which has politicians seeing the life of the citizens through tinted windows, is reminiscent of that voiced in the protest songs by the group Bell. In a recent song, the group Tatar blames the rich in general for the plight of the nation's poor:

> *The rich ones with money live like in Heaven*
> *They just play with their money and their girls and*
> *Use their money to play with other people.*
> *But the other ones, on their birthdays, must drink alcohol and water*
> *When their kids come home from school, they must eat just bread and sugar*
> *Why is it this way? Would you say that this is an equal society?*[21]

In rapping about the inequalities of life in contemporary Mongolia, these hip-hop groups appear to exemplify the sense of entitlement and insubordination that Rose identified in rap music as it spread to communities around the United States. Yet despite such apparent similarities, Mongolian rap developed in a very different cultural world than did rap of the American inner cities. The "neighborhood" of New York City bears little in common with that celebrated in the raps and videos of Mongolian hip-hop groups, and one of the key differences is the absence of institutional racism and discrimination.

RAP AND RACE IN MONGOLIA

Rose describes how the ghettos emerged in the 1970s as the city underwent a period of rapid socio-economic transformation. In this period, shrinking federal investment in the city, the decline in the availability of affordable housing, and a shift in the job market away from blue-collar manufacturing positions and towards white-collar, hit the city's new immigrant communities and its poorest residents hard.[22] Long-existing racially and ethnically mixed communities, particularly African-American and Hispanic communities, experienced the rapid disintegration of the communal bonds and social services that had long held them together, a

---

[21] Tatar, "Second Album" (n.d.)

[22] Rose, *op. cit.,* 30.

process that was made worse by the city's "renewal" projects in the same period, which transformed the physical landscape of these communities and forced many people to leave their homes. The destruction of these communities contributed to the emergence of profound social problems within them. For many people on the outside looking in, these neighborhoods became "ghettos," places of "violence and danger" that "consumes the poorest and most economically fragile communities of color."[23]

Rose goes on to describe how for the people in these troubled communities, hip-hop provided a means of reclaiming their physical neighborhood for themselves. Rapping about the everyday lives of the people in these spaces through their songs, showing the "hood" and the people who live there through their videos, and "tagging" locations as their own through their graffiti were just some of the ways in which these people could affirm their experiences and identities as residents of the ghetto. Using the "ghetto as a source of identity," Rose says, "undermines the stigma of poverty and social marginality" for the people who live there and gives them back a sense of pride and ownership.[24] It also allowed them the opportunity to critique the larger society for marginalizing them and their communities.[25]

In Ulaanbaatar, however, no such "ghetto" exists. While there are some areas of the city, for instance the *ger* districts, that are often perceived as more dangerous than others, there are no parts of the city that are widely associated with people of a particular racial, ethnic, or socio-economic class. And while some members of the new wealthy class are increasingly choosing to isolate themselves from others,[26] most Mongols of all socio-economic classes continue to live in relative proximity with each other. The mythic "classless" society of the socialist era still weighs heavily in Mongols' perception of their nation.

But the belief that Mongolia is racially and ethnically homogeneous is also widely held. While there are racial and ethnic minori-

---

23 *Ibid.*, 11.

24 *Ibid.*, 12.

25 *Ibid.*, 60.

26 This is particularly noticeable in the recent trend to build expensive condominiums behind large walled and guarded compounds.

ties living and working in the country,[27] Mongols can claim no contemporary geographical or historical continuities with racial oppression and difference as experienced within African-American communities. Yet so pronounced is this aspect of racial oppression in the discourse of global rap that some Mongolian rappers are tempted to create a historical link with it. The rapper "Skitzo" (Ankhbaatar) from the group Lumino tried to do this when he described how Mongols and African-Americans both share a similar history of oppression. "Just as the Blacks suffered under years of slavery at the hands of colonial masters in the U.S.," he says, "so too did the Mongols suffer, first under the Manchus and then at the hands of the Communists."[28] This view is both historically problematic and not widely shared among other Mongols.

The absence of a "ghetto" and any realistic historical connections with racial or ethnic oppression in Ulaanbaatar shows the problems that Mongolian rappers have had in appropriating this global popular song genre and mapping it onto the landscape of contemporary Ulaanbaatar. While they may shoot their videos in marginalized, desolate, or long forgotten locations throughout the city, they are typically generalized or virtual "hoods," bearing few identifying markers as to where they are or whose neighborhood it is. In this way, as Rose pointed out, these "ghetto" locations become mere symbols of the "authentic," a way for rappers to show their "'authenticity' and hipness."[29] Likewise, Mongolian rappers may closely imitate the 'gangsta' looks, gestures, and bodily movements associated with African-American rappers, but they do little to communicate to their Mongolian audiences what they mean and why they are using them. It is as if, after appropriating a global song form deeply invested with the discourse of race and ethnicity, Mongolian rappers have completely "erased" race and ethnicity from it.

---

[27] The Kazakhs are the largest minority in the country, but they only make up around 6% of the total population and nearly all live in the far western province of Bayan-Ölgii.

[28] Ankhbaatar, in 2004 interview. The reference to the Manchus indicates the period when "Outer Mongolia" was a part of the Qing Manchu Dynasty (1691-1911).

[29] Rose, *op. cit.,* 11.

It is because of this apparent disconnection with race that some have dismissed the entire phenomenon of rap as foreign to Mongolia. The singer Jargalsaikhan believes that rap can in no way grow in the same soil of racial oppression and poverty in Mongolia that existed in the ghettos of the United States:

> Rap music is the music of the ghettos of New York City and places like that. These kids [Mongolian rap artists] grew up in nice homes and were all well-educated. They have no roots in the conditions of life that created rap—like racism, discrimination, and a hard life. The blacks could sing this music because their blood was boiling.[30]

He adds that he's been to the United States and "seen the ghettos" of the American East where "people are always shooting each other and doing drugs,"[31] and insists that such conditions just do not exist in Mongolia.

The Mongolian rapper BAT furthers this characterization of Mongolian rappers as merely imitating African-American culture in ways similar to how actors play roles in movies:

> They must think, if we can't sing like gangsters, then let's pretend we are for our albums and videos. These guys, they dress like this here, but when you meet them on the street, do they dress like that? No! They're just middle class guys who live with their mom and dad![32]

As these views indicate, the ongoing debates about the authenticity of rap often rest on fairly essentialized views about the nature of both global rap and the experience of African-Americans in the inner city of New York. To dismiss Mongolian rap as inauthentic, however, because it cannot claim any direct connection with these experiences is also to dismiss the experience of the Mongolian youths who feel rap to be both authentic and real in their home country. Ian Maxwell (2003) writes of a similar

---

30 Jargalsaikhan, in 2004 interview.

31 *Ibid.*

32 Batbold, in 2005 interview.

situation in his study of rap in Sydney, Australia, where, as in Mongolia, he found hip-hop being maintained in communities of (often white) youths who likewise could not claim to share in "a discourse of historical continuity" with African-American rappers. Yet to label that their rap as inauthentic is, as Maxwell sees it, to ignore "genuine, phenomenological subjects, furnishing themselves and their practices, with narratives and knowledges that *they experience as genuine*, as *real*."[33]

It is in such settings that Rose's framework for the study of hip-hop as defined by the experience of Afrodiasporic cultures breaks down. We need instead to turn to the views of scholars who have studied the appropriation of hip-hop in contexts outside of the United States. Tony Mitchell finds that as hip-hop became truly global, its roots in the African-American experiences of American inner cities became less important. While hip-hop traditions as appropriated by different peoples and cultures around the world remain "undoubtedly initially influenced by U.S. hip-hop," he says, "they represent a continually shifting, heterogeneous, and complex music scene in which hip-hop is displaced and often delyricized. In the process it becomes a more amorphous, abstract, and atmospheric cross-genre musical practice, engulfing a wide range of home-grown musical and lyrical influences.[34]

While Mongolian hip-hop shares many similarities with American 'ganstarap,' it also has become, as Mitchell suggests, more of a hybrid genre that makes use of "home-grown musical and lyrical influences." Its emphasis has become "more amorphous" and "abstract." The elements of entitlement and aggressive insubordination that are evident in it have little to do with expressions of frustration of people experiencing racial oppression and poverty, and more to do with youths seeking to create a unique identity for themselves within a larger world of musical expression, one which many feel does not reflect their own unique experiences with the world into which they are growing up. Tony Mitchell found that in other parts of the world, hip-hop has become "a vehicle for global

---

[33] Ian Maxwell, *Phat Beats, Dope Rhymes: Hip-Hop Down Under Comin' Upper* (Middletown: Wesleyan University Press, 2003), 47. Italics in the original source.
[34] Tony Mitchell, "Another Root—Hip-Hop Outside the USA," 16.

youth affiliations and a tool for reworking local identities,"[35] and in a number of ways, this appears to be the case in Mongolia.

HIP-HOP AND THE VOICE OF A NEW GENERATION

A number of Mongolian rappers generally confirmed the characterizations made by Jargalsaikhan and BAT that most of them are neither poor nor racially oppressed. Rapper "Skitzo" describes the members of his group Lumino as being "all from good homes; we're not from the ghettos like the blacks of the United States."[36] In fact, many of the rap artists and groups now working in Ulaanbaatar do appear to come from the emerging middle class in society. Most have graduated from high school, some from college, and more than a few have studied art or music or traveled to the United States or Europe. Some have told me that becoming a rap artist is not something the poor in their society can do because they would need to have some capital to first create their product. One singer told me that he had to sell his car to help his group raise the money it needed to produce their first run of CDs.

Yet most of these rappers also draw a clear distinction between U.S. hip-hop and the rap music and hip-hop culture that they are seeking to create in Mongolia. Their goal, many say, is to show people that Mongolian rappers are not the thugs and criminals they may portray in their videos, but rather, as "Skitzo" puts it, that they are "real artists who lead stable lives and are part of professional bands." Mongolian rappers want their subcultural art to be taken seriously by the musical mainstream, and thus they were pleased when the Pentatonic music awards included hip-hop for the first time as one of the awards categories in 2001. That same year the Mongolian Hip-Hop Association, which seeks to promote Mongolian hip-hop domestically and internationally, received official recognition from the government. In the past few years, hip-hop has become one of the most important new markets to emerge in the popular music industry. "Now," says rapper

[35] Mitchell, *op. cit.,* 7.
[36] Ankhbaatar, in 2004 interview.

Batorgil of the group Ice Top, "there is no large show in Ulaanbaatar that will not include at least one hip-hop group. We stayed firm to our desire to bring this art to Mongolia."[37]

Just as importantly, the rappers see themselves and their audiences, most of whom range in age from their teens to early twenties, as being of a distinctly different generation from those singers and audiences that make up the musical mainstream in the country. The rapper Batbayar from the group Digital expresses his sentiment about his relationship with those of "socialist era" generations, including his parents:

> I got into rap because to me it was a way to express myself in a free way. My parents used to prohibit me from going to see hip-hop shows and hip-hop art. This was just after the socialist era, but people like them still had a socialist mentality. I didn't listen to my parents but instead followed my own ideas. It's been 10 years since I got involved with hip-hop and I'm proud that I can now make a living as a rap artist.[38]

"Skitzo" explains how his generation has grown up in a very different kind of world than did those in the generations that preceded them:

> We want to show the older generations, those in their 30s and 40s, that we are different from them. These were the generations brought up in the socialist era. These people were all taught the same things and boiled in the same sauce. Our generation likes songs that touch on reality and don't just talk about romantic love. Our generation is just now opening its eyes to see the whole world, not just Mongolia. We [Mongolian rap artists] have started a revolution in our country and we're changing the way young people are thinking.[39]

---

[37] Batorgil, in 2005 interview.

[38] Batbayar, in 2005 interview.

[39] Ankhbaatar, in 2004 interview.

CONCLUSIONS

While Mongolian rappers may borrow freely from American 'gangsta' rap traditions, what this study shows is that they subsequently use these cultural materials in entirely unique ways. Mongolian rappers are not seeking to fight against institutionalized racism and poverty, as Rose found in the rap of the American inner cities. Nor are they using the genre as a weapon of social protest against a powerful state government, as Michael Bodden found in the youth musical cultures of Indonesia in the 1990s.[40] Mongolian rappers sing about poverty and governmental corruption, but most of their songs touch on themes such as their desire to achieve personal and artistic freedom, to look at the realities of love and life with open eyes, and to be engaged with the world at large.

Rap in Mongolia is most strongly connected with a segment of the youth who have used the medium as a vehicle for defining their generational distinctiveness. These youths have effectively used rap as a means of opening spaces for their voices in the nation's popular culture and creating opportunities for them to express those traits that they believe define their unique experience in the world. In the process, they have also changed the nature of the musical mainstream. While there is still debate among some of its leading figures about the authenticity of Mongolian hip-hop, others are now embracing it. Some of the most famous Mongolian ballad singers, including Ariunaa and Sarantuya, now frequently include rapping and breakdancing in some of their songs and concerts, often inviting hip-hop groups to share the stage with them.

At the same time, in closely associating their identity with the global images of hip-hop, Mongolian rappers have also been stating their affiliation with global youth cultural movements. As this study shows, Mongolian youth are neither passive consumers nor unfortunate victims of some monolithic global cultural imperialism emanating from the West. They have their eyes sharpened and their ears pricked to pick up on interesting cultural materials wherever they originate, be they from the ghettos of the United States

[40] See his "Rap in Indonesian Youth Music of the 1990s: 'Globalization,' 'Outlaw Genres,' and Social Protest."

or a recording studio in Seoul, and they have shown themselves quite adept at appropriating these "global" materials and adapting them to their own local contexts. As the quality of their art demonstrates, Mongolian rappers are interacting with the global culture with a high degree of sophistication.

Despite its ability to rework local identities and affirm global youth affinities,[41] however, Mongolian rap continues to remain largely confined to the nation's borders. This is because the global flow of culture continues to move primarily in one direction, from the "developed" nations towards places like Mongolia. Mongolian hip-hop artists express frustration over their limited opportunities to contribute their own unique forms of hip-hop to the transnational Hip-Hop Nation. This has been a situation experienced by Mongolian popular musical artists for the past several decades. When they speak of gaining access to international markets, they are not necessarily speaking about the United States or Europe. With the development of MTV-Asia and VH1-Asia music channels in the mid-1990s, the Asian continent has emerged as an important market for popular music in its own right. Most Mongolian popular music artists include stops in Asia during their international tours and a few have even appeared on the Asian music channels. But so far none has been able to break into the popular culture world of either the developed East or West, suggesting that despite reaching even the most isolated places on Earth, these cultural flows continue to reflect some of the profound inequalities of the global marketplace.

BIBLIOGRAPHY

Appadurai, Arjun. "Disjunctures and Difference in the Global Cultural Economy," *Public Culture* 2:2 (1990), 1-24.

Bodden, Michael. "Rap in Indonesian Youth Music of the 1990s: 'Globalization,' 'Outlaw Genres,' and Social Protest," *Journal of Asian Music* 36:2 (2005), 1-26.

Hessler, Peter. "The Rap of Khan," *The Boston Globe* (7 May 2001).

---

41 Mitchell, *op. cit.,* 7.

Janzen, Joerg, et al. *A New Ger-Settlement in Ulaanbaatar: Functional Differentiation, Demographic and Socioeconomic Structure and Origin of Residents*. Ulaanbaatar: National University of Mongolia, Center for Development Research, 2002. (Research Paper no. 1).

Kristof, Nicholas D. "A Mongolian Rock Group Fosters Democracy," *The New York Times* (26 March 1990), C11:1.

Marsh, Peter K. *The Horse-head Fiddle and the Cosmopolitan Reimagination of Tradition in Mongolia*. New York: Routledge, 2006.

Maxwell, Ian. *Phat Beats, Dope Rhymes: Hip-Hop Down Under Comin' Upper*. Middletown: Wesleyan University Press, 2003.

Mitchell, Tony. "Another Root—Hip-Hop outside the USA." In *Global Noise: Rap and Hip-Hop Outside the USA*, ed. Tony Mitchell. Middletown: Wesleyan University Press, 2002.

Ramet, Sabrina Petra, ed. *Rocking the State*. Boulder: Westview Press, 1994.

Rose, Tricia. *Black Noise: Rap Music and Black Culture in Contemporary America*. Middletown: Wesleyan University Press, 1994.

Ryback, Timothy W. *Rock Around the Bloc: A History of Rock Music in Eastern Europe and the Soviet Union*. New York: Oxford University Press, 1990.

Starr, S. Frederick. *Red and Hot. The Fate of Jazz in the Soviet Union*. New York: Oxford University Press, 1983.

Troitsky, Artemy. *Back in the USSR*. London: Faber and Faber, 1987.

RECORDINGS

Black Rose, "Tengeriin Tamga," Moritkhangai Company CD 3401 (2001)

Dain ba Enkh, "Neg Chig," Ritm Studio (2002)

Digital, "This Is Life," Michid Records (2003)

Ice Top, New Life," Star Studios (n.d.)

Lumino, "Ireed butssan khair mini – Special Edition," Michig Records (2003)

Snep Crew, "Jin Tan Tsomog," Michid Records (2004)

Tatar, "Second Album," Sonor Records, n.d.

INTERVIEWS

Ankhbaatar, D., Ulaanbaatar, Mongolia (September 13, 2004)
Batbayar, D., Ulaanbaatar, Mongolia (July 4, 2005)
Batbold, B., Ulaanbaatar, Mongolia (July 4, 2005)
Batorgil, J., Ulaanbaatar, Mongolia (June 27, 2005)
Hurd, Ulaanbaatar, Mongolia (May 15, 1999)
Jargalsaikhan, D., Ulaanbaatar, Mongolia (March 16, 1999)
________, Ulaanbaatar, Mongolia (September 26, 2004)

The Effects of Globalization on Youth in Mongolia

Bayartsetseg Terbish

In the era of globalization, a general question facing Mongolia is not whether globalization is good or bad, but how we could benefit from it and how we should prioritize our personal choices to account for the realities of a new era. From a positive perspective, globalization has been a process of the social, political, legal and economic integration of all countries, resulting in policies, technologies and institutions that make our world a better place to live in. However, sometimes globalization seems to be a force shaped by the developed countries and beneficial only for those countries and individuals with money and power. This limitation is not only apparent in the political arena but also visible in the lives of youth. Therefore, as a young individual, it was interesting for me to try to distinguish what are the positive and negative effects of globalization in the lives of young people in Mongolia.

This paper will start off with some statistics about the youth population in Mongolia, and then will share some personal observations and thoughts about the positive and negative effects of globalization on the lives of young people in Mongolia. In particular, the paper will describe challenges that are keeping many young Mongols from succeeding and using globalization to their own advantage.

According to the Mongolian National Statistical Office, 22.4% of the total population is between the ages of 15-24.[1] In the World

---

[1] Mongolia, National Statistical Office. *Statistical Yearbook*. www.nso.mn. Accessed July 9, 2004.

Fact Book 2005, it is noted that the median age of the overall population in Mongolia is 24.28 years, where the male population median age was 23.93 and female population median age was 24.64. Fadzillah emphasizes that "when it comes to globalization or transnational connections youth cultures are in the forefront of theoretical interest; youth, their ideas and commodities move easily across national borders, shaping and being shaped by all kinds of structures and meanings."[2] Based on the above population statistics, it is highly likely that more young people are experiencing the effects of globalization than Mongols in any other ten-year age group.

POSITIVE AND NEGATIVE EFFECTS OF GLOBALIZATION

During the current period of democratization and modernization, young individuals in Mongolia are striving hard to master high-tech communication skills in order to keep themselves updated with what is happening around the world. Internet and other audio and visual techniques have become some of the basic skills that help them to succeed in a competitive job market. The letter "E" has become very important in doing business, banking, trading, studying and even finding a life partner.

I remember that in my childhood the list of "do's" was considerably shorter than the one for "don't's". A part of my culture kept me in a restrictive frame and never allowed me to ask questions of adults outside of that frame. As a reward, I was praised and grew up to be a good modest girl. Now, however, as one of the consequences of globalization, this cultural modesty seems to have become outdated. Young individuals are becoming more open-minded and assertive in their demands to know about global issues. For example, young Mongols started to celebrate Global Youth Service Day and to communicate online with different

---

[2] I. Fadzillah, "The Amway connection: How transnational ideas of beauty and money affect Northern Thai girls' perceptions of their future options," in *Youthscapes: The Popular, the National, the Global,* Sunaina Maira and Elisabeth Soep, eds. (Philadelphia: University of Pennsylvania Press, 2005), 86.

youth groups in other countries in order to exchange their ideas on critical issues such as children's rights. Within Mongolia, young people are routinely expressing their ideas and concerns to government officials through online communications systems.

At the same time, we should not overlook the negative effects that globalization has had on Mongolian youth. Young people in my country ignore their original cultural values, disregard the value of the family, oppress each other and dismiss their family heritage. Mongolian cultural values are becoming difficult to identify, especially among the youth, when they are heavily influenced by Western cultural norms. By the West I mean such things as American films which project positive images of the "American Dream" and of America as a great power, through which the most common images of the West by Mongolian youth are basically formed. Once a young mind is influenced by Western positivism, it is more likely that the traditional cultural values will be veiled and more and more youth will wish to live abroad.

Young Mongolian girls' perceptions of their female identity and expectations are shaped by the influence of globalization and they are filled with a desire to be fashion models. For teenage girls, models of globalization encourage them to take on more adult-like roles at an early age. For young female adults, this approach has caused an increase in the divorce rate and a lack of appreciation of male partners. For example, working as beauty product distributors for multinational companies like Oriflame has given girls more competence to participate in the labor force and, at the same time, gave them increased confidence to fulfill their wish to become a cosmopolitan model of attractiveness through even such means as cosmetic surgery. This attitude may possibly be one of the many sources of conflict that have led to family divorce because many men are not ready to support female empowerment due to deep-rooted concepts of patriarchal power in Mongolia. For instance, in 1989, the divorce rate was 1.6% but this percentage increased to 2.7% in 2004, which could possibly be linked to increased female capacities and expectations.[3]

---

[3] Ministry of Labor and Social Welfare, & UNFPA. *Current Situation of Families.* Ulaanbaatar, 2004.

Nowadays, the mass media in Mongolia bombard the young people with their Westernized broadcasts, which are mostly imitations of popular programs that attract youth interest in the West. Young people learn about diverse musical genres, trends in modern fashions and new products through the media and they feel connected to the rest of the world through popular programs and channels such as MTV. However, as mentioned above, the ideas of youth and their preferences move easily across national borders. It would be hard to find a common language to communicate with young people if you wanted to talk about traditional folk songs or games with them. Rather, the hot topic to discuss would be the latest hip-hop hits, Hollywood movie releases or how to tear my jeans in order to make them more fashionable.

This approach results in oppression and discrimination among the young population. For instance, those who listen to traditional music and who do not prefer funky clothing might be called awkward, old-fashioned or geeky. As a personal example, not long ago my nephew asked me to send him the most modern and coolest clothes, otherwise he would find it hard to be accepted into the circle of boys in his class. Teachers and parents seem unable to see the connection between oppression and low self-esteem in their children, assuming that low self-esteem is a natural characteristic of modest children. Some acute social problems that might occur due to this phenomenon are marginalization and even increased rates of suicide based on low self-esteem.

Traditionally, the parenting style in Mongolia has been more authoritarian than in the West. Children are taught to accept restrictive and limited opportunities and do what their parents want them to do. This tendency probably has led to increased arguments between parents and their children when the parents' wish to follow the traditional heritage collides with the preferences of modern youth. All too often the result has been that parents see their children as being disobedient and the children view their parents as misusing parental authority.[4]

[4]S.P. Robbins, P. Chaterjee, and R.E. Canda, *Contemporary Human Behavior Theory: Critical Perspective for Social Work* (Boston: Allyn & Bacon, 1998).

This rising tension between parents and their children has in not a few cases been exacerbated by religion where parents and their children belong to different religions. It seems that our society is not ready to accept and respect the difference in individual religious beliefs, especially the youth's belief in Christianity, even though it is stated in the constitution that individuals have freedom of conscience and religion. For example, many young people claim that the main cause of family arguments was parental disrespect and disagreement towards their belief in Christianity.

CHALLENGES FACING YOUTH

There is a huge gap of income inequality in our country which creates a challenge for youth to experience the positive effects of globalization equally. Youth from wealthier family have a greater advantage in using of what globalization has to offer in the information and technology sectors, while youth from poor families are left behind. Some of us enjoy driving fancy cars and get the latest information online while others have never even touched a computer screen.

Inequality is closely related to another challenge, which is urban and rural disparity. Many young and talented individuals do not have equal opportunities to benefit from the globalization process, in particular in rural Mongolia, because of poor infrastructure and isolated places of residence. For those who live in urban areas, the world is a small place thanks to internet sites, news and calling cards, which help them keep connected to everything they want. But this is only one side of the coin. Young people living in rural areas lack the opportunities to know what is happening in the rest of the world, when there are only few channels of information open to them.

CONCLUSION

In summary, globalization has both positive and negative effects on youth life in Mongolia. Most of the effects seem to be as inseparable as two sides of a coin and it is extremely difficult to judge today whether globalization offers mainly positive or negative effects. This is because Mongolia has still a long way to go in order to see the full effects of globalization. Positively, globalization provides accessibility to technological advancements and internet products. It also helps us to understand the importance of learning languages and it influences us to develop ourselves intellectually with a motivation of learning more. Therefore, it is crucial for our country to distinguish between the positive and negative effects of globalization and see to it that the positive impacts affect all young people equally.

Negatively, globalization has influenced youth to disregard the values of forming a family, ignore their traditional cultural values in favor of Western attractions that are offered through media, oppress each other and come into conflict with their family heritage. Youth living in rural areas, preserving our nomadic way of life, are a valuable segment of our cultural background and they have their own chances to make a decision about whether they would prefer to be "modernized" or continue their nomadic way of living. The question remaining, which has not been answered is "In which direction is the modern youth culture in Mongolia heading?"

BIBLIOGRAPHY

Fadzillah, I. "The Amway connection: How transnational ideas of beauty and money affect Northern Thai girls' perceptions of their future options." In *Youthscapes : The Popular, the National, the Global,* Sunaina Maira and Elisabeth Soep, eds. (Philadelphia : University of Pennsylvania Press, 2005), 85-102.

Mongolia. Ministry of Labor and Social Welfare, & UNFPA. *Current situation of families.* Ulaanbaatar, 2004.

Mongolia. National Statistical Office. *Statistical Yearbook.* In www.nso.mn.

Robbins, S.P., P. Chaterjee, and R.E. Canda. *Contemporary Human Behavior Theory: Critical Perspective for Social Work.* Boston: Allyn & Bacon, 1998.

About the Authors

Shagdaryn Bira is a member of the Mongolian Academy of Sciences since its inception in 1960, the Secretary-General of the International Association for Mongol Studies. He is a member of the UNESCO Scientific Committee for writing the History of Civilizations of Central Asia and of the Mongolian National Commission for UNESCO. He authored numerous books and more than 100 articles on Mongolian medieval history and traditional culture, Buddhism in Mongolia, and its linkages with Central Asian countries, including India and Tibet. He was awarded Mongolia's highest academic title, Honored Science Worker of Mongolia. He is a laureate of the National Prize of Mongolia and a honorary member of the International Academy of Indian Culture, Honorary Professor of Inner Mongolia University, Honorary Doctor of Moscow State University of International Relations, Honorary Member of the Central Eurasian Studies Society, and a member of the New York Academy of Sciences. He was awarded the Denis Sinor Medal of the Royal Asiatic Society of Great Britain and Ireland.

Paul D. Buell is an Adjunct Professor at Western Washington University. He is a co-author of *A Soup for the Qan : Chinese Dietary Medicine of the Mongol Era as Seen in Hu Szu-Hui's Yin-shan cheng-yao* (2000), author of *Historical Dictionary of the Mongol World Empire* (2003) and of more than 100 other books, book chapters and articles. He is currently contributing to a comparative history of the horse and veterinary medicine in China. His specialties are the history of the Mongolian empire, comparative medical history, modern Central Asian politics and culture, and maritime history. His co-author, **Ngan Le**, was born in Vietnam and is currently an undergraduate majoring in economics at the University of Washington. She plans to become an art critic and has worked on the influence of Goethe's color theories on modern art in addition to hunger in Mongolia.

Alicia J. Campi is the president of the U.S.-Mongolia Advisory Group, the first consultancy company devoted to educational, environmental, technological, and tourist development in Mongolia. She is also the president of the Chinggis Khan Foundation and a member of the Board of Directors of the Mongolia Society. She has authored over fifty speeches, articles, and book chapters. She served as a Foreign Service officer for thirteen years in Asia, including Mongolia, and has travelled to Mongolia twenty-two times.

Mei-hua Lan received her Ph.D. in Inner Asian and Altaic Studies from Harvard University in 1996 with a dissertation entitled *Mongolian Independence Movement of 1911: A Pan-Mongolian Endeavor* and is currently Associate Professor at National Chengchi University in Taiwan. She specializes in modern Mongolian history and offers several courses concerning written Mongolian, Inner Asian history, and ethnic relations. She is also the author of the book *Relations Between Outer Mongolia and China Under Tsedenbal, 1952-1984* (2000, in Chinese).

Peter K. Marsh is the resident director of the American Center for Mongolian Studies in Ulaanbaatar. He is a member of the Board of Directors of the Mongolia Society and author of *The Horse-head Fiddle and the Cosmopolitan Reimagination of Mongolia* (to be published in 2006). The current focus of his research is on the interplay between rural and urban musical traditions in Mongolia as part of broader historical trends towards nationalization and modernization.

Henry G. Schwarz is Professor Emeritus of Western Washington University. He currently serves as the president of the Mongolia Society and as vice-president of the International Association for Mongol Studies. He founded the Center for East Asian Studies in 1970 and the Mongolia Program in 1975 at Western Washington University. He is the author of numerous books, including *Mongolian Short Stories* (1974), *Bibliotheca Mongolica* (1978), *The Minorities of Northern China: A Survey* (1984), *An Uyghur-English Dictionary* (1992), *Mongolia and the Mongols: Holdings at Western Washington University* (1993) as well as many book chapters and articles.

Bayartsetseg Terbish is currently a Master's candidate in the George Warren Brown School of Social Work of Washington University in St. Louis.